W9-BZI-588

International boundary
State boundary
• City
☆ State capital
★ National capital
▲ Ancient Mayan city
MayaQuest route

DZIBILCHALTUN
Mérida ☆ START
Cancún
CHICHÉN ITZÁ
COBA
Cozumel
UXMAL
Yucatán
LABNA
TULÚM
Campeche ☆
Quintana Roo
Bay of Campeche
Campeche
BECÁN
XPUJ IL
Chetumal ☆
CHICANA
HORMIGUERO
CALAKMUL
Hondo River
Caribbean Sea
Tabasco
Villahermosa ☆
EL MIRADOR
RIO AZUL
Belize River
Belize City
PALENQUE
END
Belmopan ★
Usumacinta River
TIKAL
XUNANTUNICH
Chiapas
YAXCHILÁN
Lake
Petén Itza
BELIZE
Tuxtla
Gutiérrez ☆
BONAMPAK
CARACOL
Sarstún River
GUATEMALA
San Pedro Sula •
Lake
Izabal
QUIRIGUA
N
W E
S
Quezaltenango •
Copán •
HONDURAS
Motagua River
Guatemala ☆
Tegucigalpa ★
0      50      100 miles
San
Salvador ★
EL
SALVADOR
NICARAGUA
0    50    100 kilometers
PACIFIC OCEAN

MEXICO

# MAYAQUEST

*The Interactive Expedition*

For Sam—

A master scholar, an eloquent wordsmith and all around good guy. Thanks for helping make MayaQuest a success.

Pedals Up!

6-18-96

# MAYA QUEST

## The Interactive Expedition

Dan Buettner

Photos by
Douglas Mason & Dan Buettner

Foreword by
David Freidel

ONION
PRESS

*For Rafi*
*who graciously*
*endures my expeditions*

Onion Press, Inc.
4110 Nicollet Avenue South
Minneapolis, MN 55409

Printed in Hong Kong

**Publisher's Cataloging in Publication**

Buettner, Dan.
     MayaQuest : the interactive
expedition / Dan Buettner ; photographs
by Douglas Mason and Dan Buettner.
          p. cm.
          Includes index.
          ISBN 0-9640334-2-9

     1. Buettner, Dan--Journeys--
Central America. 2. Central America--
Description and travel. 3. Cycling--
Central America. 4. Internet (Computer
network).  I. Mason, Douglas.  II. Title.

F1433.2.B84 1996      917.28
                              QBI95-20874

*Design and production*
David J. Farr, *ImageSmythe*

*Copyeditor*
Jean M. Cook

*Endsheet map*
Patrica Isaacs, *Parrot Graphics*

*Computer glyph*
Nancy Wirsig McClure,
*Hand to Mouse Arts*

*Prepress*
Digital Pre-Press International through
PrintNet

*Printing and Binding*
Paramount Printing through PrintNet

# CONTENTS

Some years ago, Tony Andrews, a friend of mine and a Maya archaeologist who grew up in Yucatán, told me this story. He said he happened to be at the Maya site of Tikal, a vast and famous ruin in the Petén rain forest of Guatemala, when a film crew showed up with a request to shoot the pyramids. The local authorities didn't speak English, and the crew didn't speak Spanish, so Tony ended up translating for everybody. The crew was filming for *Star Wars*. The authorities wanted to know what the film was about, so the production crew explained how the pyramids of Tikal were on a jungle moon circling a desert planet in a faraway galaxy, the base of rebel forces intent on destroying the imperial death star against all odds. Skipping such bizarre details, Tony told the site officials in Spanish that the film would be seen everywhere in the world and that it would help make Tikal famous. He was, of course, telling the truth. For just about everyone who watches films has seen the pyramids of Tikal with rebel space fighters flying from them to heroically engage the evil empire.

The imagination of modern movie storytellers can't rival what the Maya actually did in and thought of their world — a world full of gods, heroes, and demons, beautiful and ghastly, pictured in graceful, confident art. They have fascinated Americans for a century and a half, ever since the journalist John L. Stephens and the artist Stephen Catherwood published their pictures and accounts of lost cities in the tropical forests of Mexico and Central America in a series of bestsellers. Occupying a region about the size of New Mexico and numbering in the millions during their Classic period (300–900 A.D.), the lowland Maya literally reached for the stars. They were expert astronomers, devising calendars of great accuracy and mapping the cycles of the sun, moon, Milky Way, constellations, and planets. They invented the concept of zero and place notation mathematics — well beyond the capacities of the contemporary Romans. They developed a true writing system that encoded their spoken languages, and they carved elegant texts on the stone monuments that graced their cities. PreColumbian Maya texts constitute the only real literature left to us from before the time of the European conquests. In architecture, the Maya invented a form of concrete construction in the northern lowlands that allowed them to sheath palaces in beautiful stone mosaic decoration. Frank Lloyd Wright regarded the resulting architectural designs among the finest ever conceived anywhere, at any time. Practical and ingenious as well as artistic, the lowland Maya managed the fragile soils of the tropics for thousands of years to yield not only sufficient food for large populations but also surplus crops of cacao and cotton to trade abroad. Their commerce with peoples beyond their kingdoms made them wealthy in jade, precious shell, obsidian, and other imported goods. Theirs was truly one of the magnificent ancient civilizations of the world.

The mystery of the Maya is why so many of their wondrous cities lay ruined and abandoned when the Spanish came to their lands. Archaeologists now know that Classic Maya civilization experienced a catastrophe in the ninth century A.D. Not all Maya lands were devastated, but the great — cut a broad swath across the base of the Yucatán peninsula, 80,000 square kilometers in extent and sweeping through dozens of states. Even for tough-minded scientific archaeologists, this enigma holds a special allure and presents a major challenge to their detective skills in revealing what really happened in the past of our world. There are many reasonable hypotheses to explain this collapse, reasonable because they can be tested against evidence excavated, measured, sampled, and analyzed from the Maya ruins and ambient countryside.

MayaQuest posed this main question to explore with the classrooms and other online participants: What happened to the Maya civilization in the ninth century A.D. to cause the great collapse and abandonment of hundreds of cities, towns, and villages? Like all really good questions, this one has no single, simple answer, but rather invites contemplation of the whole range of challenges facing big and complicated societies — ours included. Was it a population problem? Maybe the Maya eventually could not produce enough food given their kind of agriculture and their land. Was it a natural catastrophe? Maybe droughts, locusts, volcanic explosions, hurricanes, earthquakes, or plagues brought down the Classic period of the Maya. Perhaps strife, warfare, or rebellion of commoners against the elite caused the collapse. It might strike one as depressing or even unfair to focus on a civilization's collapse; we usually think about golden ages instead. But even after more than a century of thinking about the Maya, both the public and the experts remain fascinated with the abandonment of their cities, lost in time, their towering pyramids enthralled in vibrant green jungle like Sleeping Beauty's castle. Besides, abuse of tropical rain forest, population pressure, war—these are real and apparent dangers of our world worth considering even at the safe distance of a thousand or more years.

Most experts on the ancient Maya will hedge their bets when asked what happened in the great collapse. They usually point out that with a population numbering in the millions, maintaining food needs with Stone Age farming technology was very difficult. Add ever-increasing demands for more work, more tribute from a burgeoning aristocracy, regional warfare, and periodic drought and you have a potent recipe for disaster. At the same time, experts on the Maya past do have strong, often differing, opinions as to which of these problems sped the vicious cycle of afflictions to the crisis of abandonment. Crisis is fairly common in the history of civilization; outright collapse and abandonment of a whole region covering tens of thousands of square kilometers is unusual and worth explaining.

For example, T. Patrick Culbert looks at the mounting evidence from ongoing field exploration and survey throughout Maya country for an extraordinarily large and dense population—up to 200 people per square kilometer overall—in the Late Classic period (600–900 A.D.), and he sees a population bomb that any number of other problems could have eas-

ily detonated. But from the vantage of the city of Caracol in Belize, Arlen Chase sees a final phase of civilization that dates after the collapse for a century or more. At the citadel of Xunantunich, also in Belize, Richard Leventhal and Wendy Ashmore also think this community survived the collapse by opting out of regional conflicts and politics. The MayaQuest team talked to Arlen and Diane Chase at Caracol and Wendy Ashmore at Xunantunich, about their research and reported online. These archaeologists have to wonder whether perhaps the collapse was politically and militarily selective in ways that belie a pervasive population bomb hypothesis. It's true that parts of Belize, most of the northern Maya lowlands, and the southern Maya highlands of Guatemala never did experience the ninth century collapse— whatever other crises they endured.

Glyphic Maya history declares that civil war between regional royal alliances drove the Maya to the brink of social chaos in the eighth century. Arthur Demarest and his team at Dos Pilas, Guatemala, documented, through defensive parapets, ruins, and destruction, that war indeed was a terrible force as the great collapse loomed before the civilization. When the team passed through Dos Pilas, everything was quiet and buried, and they were more impressed with the contemporary conflicts in the area and the general aura of poverty in this part of Maya country. Demarest ran a huge program there in southwestern Petén, Guatemala, with many scientists looking for evidence that the Maya had abused their environment or overpopulated the farmland in ways that might have caused collapse. No such evidence could be found; all his discoveries pointed to warfare as the major problem in this case. The

texts paralleled the archaeology: Demarest found the broken throne in the main palace at Dos Pilas. Epigraphers translated a monument celebrating final victory over Dos Pilas at a nearby site, exulting in the destruction of the royal throne.

In contrast to Demarest's team in the Petexbatun region, Don and Pru Rice found clear evidence for stress on the environment by the eighth century, through their surveys of sites around lakes in central Petén and their systematic study of the ancient environment from lake core samples. The landscape they envision on the eve of the collapse is one of exhausted farm fields, dwindling forest reserves, a society stymied in the face of insurmountable challenges to feed itself. Richard Hansen adds to the gloomy picture with evidence that the ninth century witnessed severe droughts, registered in the dramatic lowering of water levels in Lake Petén-Itzá. Scientists working with lake deposits in the northern lowlands recently found more evidence for a period of major drought in the ninth century. Drought means crop failure, and crop failure can mean famine in an agricultural society. Whatever the local variations, the Maya were experiencing environmental stress in parts of the lowlands.

Other kinds of problems are harder to detect archaeologically. Some analyses of human remains suggest a deteriorating quality of nutrition for ordinary people and even elite in such royal capitals as Copán in Honduras, Tikal, and Altar de Sacrificios in Guatemala, all of which experienced the collapse. But some diseases that might have caused population decline do not register on bones. I helped excavate a pit of about fifty men, women, and children who died after contact with Europeans and were hastily buried together in a ceremonial center on Cozumel Island.

*Pyramids at Tikal.*

That was probably a result of introduced disease. Archaeologists have not reported such clear evidence of epidemic death elsewhere in Maya country. The volcano El Chorchon in Chiapas, which blanketed the city of Palenque with ash in 1982, evidently erupted during the Classic period as well. But it is hard to pin major disruptions of the regional society on this kind of localized disaster. Hurricanes are terrifying and periodically devastating for large parts of Maya country. But people today resolutely recover from such destruction within a few years, and they probably did in the past. Earthquakes could have hit some Maya cities, such as Quirigua in Guatemala or Copán in Honduras, but the great majority of the cities that collapsed were not in the zone of terrible earthquake damage. It is not that the ancient Maya did not respect the destructive power of nature or illness—on the contrary, they wrote about it in their prophetic histories, the Books of Chilam Balam in Yucatán. It is just that these problems generally afflicted people across local areas or during short periods of time.

For my own part, I think that the Maya themselves provided clues to the collapse through their writings during the Classic period. The Maya are the only indigenous Americans to have left a written record in their own language recording major historical events. But how do archaeologists know whether what the Maya of 1,500 years ago wrote in their texts really reflects what was going on in their world? I debated this matter with other online experts writing on MayaQuest, for many archaeologists remain skeptical that we can get at the actuality behind public pronouncements that are bound to favor the views of royal patrons. But I look at elite historical texts in relation to archaeological facts. At the beginning of the quest, the team went to Yaxuná in Yucatán, where my crew has excavated a small stone palace that I believe was deliberately and ceremonially destroyed by enemy warriors from nearby Chichén Itzá. Through painstaking mapping of the debris in the palace, smashed pottery, layers of charcoal from bonfires, holes chopped through plaster floors, scattered bits of

human bone, and weapons, we are starting to define what deliberate destruction levels in Maya sites look like—not just at Yaxuná, but all over the region. Other archaeologists have seen such deposits before, but they did not have war in mind, so they just called them the trash of slovenly squatters living in the abandoned palaces after the collapse. But no modern Maya are as squalid in their living habits as these ancient deposits suggest. In fact, the Maya are clean-living folk who bathe regularly and keep their homes free of trash. Classic-period Maya kings say in their texts they "burned," "chopped," or "ruined" important enemy places, and I think victorious warriors really did that.

The ancient texts give us a glimpse of a complex Classic period political landscape. They reveal the Maya kings who actually built the pyramids at Tikal featured in the *Star Wars* scenes. Those holy lords probably would have been a bit perplexed by the movie version of their city, for they themselves were the imperial rulers in the Maya lowlands of 700 A.D. and later. But indeed, they were fighting great wars and prevailing against all odds. These were genuine ancient American heroes and statesmen. Hasaw-Kan-K'awil, Battle-Standard-Spirit, built the main pyramids at Tikal. This man redeemed his people and his country. At one critical juncture in centuries-long wars pitting grand alliances against each other, he had to choose between marshalling his troops southward to attack Balah-Kan-K'awil, the hated cousin king who had tortured and killed his father, or wheeling northward to engage the enemy behind the enemy, the Gatherer of Thrones, the leader of the alliance that had fought his people for generations. He turned northward, and history turned with him as he defeated, captured, and sacrificed Icha'k-K'ak', Fire-Paw, the Holy Vision-Serpent Lord of Calakmul. From the Maya vantage, war and the struggle for regional government were certainly part of the problem, and perhaps part of the hoped-for solution to crisis, on the eve of the great collapse.

People online with MayaQuest got to decide which of these different problems they most wanted the team to investigate, opting through the vote for warfare. They also studied the collapse in the context of forest ecology, weather, geography, and the basic strategies of dirt archaeology. They asked the team, archaeologists in the field, and online experts questions about the collapse and gave answers of their own based on class discussion and research. The fact is, a lot more people know about the ancient Maya today than a year ago, thanks to Dan Buettner and his many collaborators in MayaQuest.

Questing is the proper way to describe a stranger's travel through Maya country in Mexico and Central America. The Maya sages often quested paths in the lowlands and beyond their borders to bring back knowledge and valuable new things to their towns and villages. MayaQuest put teachers and children on the Maya path, along with the adults who found the quest and followed it on their own. Virtual may be the name of the medium, but this was a real-world adventure into a faraway place and time. Sitting before their bright screens, flying through cyberspace in ways the ancient Maya kings, with their magic farseeing mirrors, would have appreciated the online audience in more than 42,000 classrooms biked the path of the Maya with Dan and the team for a hundred days. Now they know that these native Americans have a past of people, not just ruins—

heroes and villains, triumphs and tragedies, governments and ordinary folk cast within a vision of the world that is both different and intriguing. They know that the contemporary Maya are a hospitable and decent people. They also know the unvarnished truth that the Maya today are struggling to survive and cope in national societies that do not value the contemporary cultures of their indigenous peoples.

Dan Buettner first outlined MayaQuest for me at the Maya Glyph Workshop in Austin, Texas, a noisy, exciting annual gathering where Mayanists argue and brainstorm about art, ancient history, archaeology, and especially the Maya writing system. I told him I wasn't going to be in Yucatán when he planned to go there, but that I thought MayaQuest was a terrific idea and a great opportunity to teach the online audience about a past civilization in this part of the world. Most important, I said, it was an opportunity to provide Americans with a glimpse of the contemporary Maya descendants of the famous ancient Maya. I did not hear much about MayaQuest after that until the prodigious work of putting together sponsors, the online program, experts, and teachers was just about complete. One reason I hadn't been tuned in is that I had just come online with the Internet in the fall of 1994. Frankly, the success of MayaQuest in getting put together is more of a mystery and a miracle to me than the raising of the Maya pyramids. Like them, MayaQuest is testimony to what happens when you have enough charisma, sweat, and imagination. I was lucky to be the keynote speaker in Minneapolis for workshops orienting teachers to MayaQuest just before Dan and the team headed out. After meeting with Dan, his family, and the many people working with him, I was

hooked. Violating some of Dan's good planning and protocol, I soon found myself online among the experts commenting on the quest and answering questions from the online audience.

Timing could not have been better for MayaQuest and the children in class to tackle the Maya collapse. Right now several major expeditions in the field are making discoveries that bear directly on the fall of important Maya kingdoms. The team got to visit several of these projects and talk to the archaeologists while they were excavating at major Classic period capitals. At the same time, people like Linda Schele, who participated online with several of her graduate students, are making exciting new breakthroughs in decoding ancient Maya texts. The decipherment of Maya glyphic writing now is allowing us to understand many declarations on stone and stucco monuments. The online audience got to be with the team at Caracol, in Belize, when epigrapher Nikolai Grube revealed the meaning of an important new text about a king who had to flee his capital for several months during an invasion by enemies. The image of that monumental text went online, marking the fastest report ever of a major Maya discovery. These texts give clues about what Maya kings, queens, and nobles were concerned with and what their governments were doing during the centuries leading up to the collapse. According to their own words, the Maya rulers were forging alliances with distant kingdoms by royal marriages. They were traveling on state visits and participating in great public festivals at which they danced and exchanged precious gifts of beautiful craft work. And they were fighting severe and protracted wars on behalf of grand alliances ruled by kings who declared themselves to be lords over the others.

*David Freidel (far left), Dan Buettner (left).*

Earlier, online participants could practically taste the dust and feel the heat as the team pushed through eastern Petén, the heart of Maya civilization, in a time of drought. A rich and lively online discussion paralleled their progress, detailing the other conditions that might have pushed the cities to collapse—drought, disease, earthquakes, devastating storms, and volcanic dust clouds among them. The problems the Maya faced probably varied from area to area, but the consensus among the seventeen archaeologists whom the team got to question in the field held that some combination of factors must have caused the collapse in each case. During the course of the quest, members of the online audience regularly logged on with their own conclusions to these thorny questions, often based on classroom debates and discussions. The later responses by children showed just how much they had thought about the Maya during this adventure, and how much they had learned about complex answers to complex, real-world questions.

They also learned about the living Maya. There are between four million and six million people who speak one of the twenty-five persisting Maya languages as a mother tongue, making the Maya, after the Quechua descendants of the Inca Empire in South America, the second largest native American group in the hemisphere. The team spent time in Yaxuná village, where I work, and got to know the mayor and the shaman, and got to enjoy the hospitality of a farming community. The

Yucatec-speaking Maya of the northern lowlands are one of the larger groups, about half a million, and the team traveled southward through several more villages like Yaxuná, bringing thousands of Americans in the online audience into Maya homes. I am often asked by people here, "What happened when the Maya disappeared?" Quite a number of Americans think that when the Maya abandoned their magnificent cities they left the region entirely. The members of the online audience who participated in MayaQuest know better and won't forget it.

Life is pretty hard for the modern Maya. They are, mostly, simple farmers and craft folk under the pressure of poverty, national policies, and proselytizing religions to forget their ancestral ways. War, for many of them, is not some distant past or intellectual abstraction. As the team biked through highland Guatemala, Dan's dispatches described orphaned children whose parents have died or disappeared in the drawn-out conflict between the army and rebels, a conflict that has left more than 100,000 Guatemalans—mostly Maya—dead or missing. But the Maya also are resilient and determined people. Just after MayaQuest ended, one online expert, Linda Schele, took a group of Americans on tour among living Maya of highland Guatemala—friends she has worked with for years now, teaching glyphic writing and learning modern wisdom. They were welcomed into Maya homes, saw Maya celebrations and sacred places, and were embraced by the warmth

and generosity of an ancient people. Don Florentin, a sage and shaman, accompanied them to see the landscape of his K'iche' ancestors. The K'iche' Maya of the central highlands, for example, are a half-million strong and still preserve their cultural heritage in Guatemala's highlands. Their Book of Council, the Popol Vuh, is not only an important reference for archaeologists but a living document. One teacher participating in MayaQuest, Peter Knopf, and his students put several parts of the Popol Vuh history of the K'iche' online for everybody. It is just one more testimonial to the fact that the collapse was not the end of the Maya world.

I think that MayaQuest will endure, too. The team is back, with a mass of beautiful photographs, films, and indelible memories of hard roads and new friends. But MayaQuest is in the minds and experiences of all the thousands of children, teachers, and interested adults who joined it. And it is online for anyone to contemplate now. The politicians and civic leaders in our country who worry about this new electronic medium of communication should take a look at this successful experiment in education. This is not virtual reality, it is as real as nonfiction books, newspapers, journals, documentary television, radio, film, and so on, but with the potential dynamism of conversation and dialogue. Children in the United States are communicating online with children in Maya country now. MayaQuest challenged members of the online audience to think about the world they are a part of in new ways; all of us who participated have grown because of it. Questing, in the context of well-organized and intelligently conceived programs such as this one, is a reaching out to their world by people who need to know about it.

Shortly after sunrise on the eighth day of May 1995, we climb the nine tiers of Palenque's Temple of the Inscriptions. From where we stand, seven ancient buildings, mired in milky haze, rise out of an impossibly green plateau like leviathan palaces in a child's dreamscape. Facing east, our septuagenarian friend, the sage Don Moises Morales, fans his arm along the horizon in a sweeping gesture that seems to encompass the entire Maya area, a 550-by-350-mile tract of Central America that stretches from northern Yucatán to northern Honduras and spans the isthmus. It is out there, among tropical forests that mask exceedingly inhospitable terrain, that one of the greatest civilizations appeared, flourished, and collapsed 600 years before the first European stepped foot on the continent. "I have been studying the Maya for thirty-seven years," Don Moises remarks quietly, almost to himself, "only to realize that I know nothing."

For the past three months, we had been exploring the Maya area by bicycle with a team including Mayanist Julie Acuff, photographer Doug Mason, and my two brothers, Steve and Nick. We had been searching for clues to better understand the ancient Maya collapse—perhaps our hemisphere's greatest mystery. It's an important mystery, because the shock wave it created more than a thousand years ago has rippled through the centuries and resonates in today's headlines. The questions in and around the Maya ruins continue to inspire—and perplex—our brightest scientists and historians.

With MayaQuest, we sought not to find the answers surrounding the collapse (that would be highly unlikely) but to directly engage an interested public and enable them to seek the answers for themselves.

My first glimpse of the Maya world came in 1987 on my way to Tierra del Fuego, Argentina, during a 15,536-mile record-setting bike ride that began in Prudhoe Bay, Alaska. My route through Guatemala had traced the Pacific coast until I read Aldous Huxley's description of Lake Atitlan as "beyond the permissibly picturesque." On a lark, I turned inland and climbed into the cool pine-

*The MayaQuest team at Calakmul ruins, (left to right) Julie Acuff, Steve Buettner, Dan Buettner, and Nick Buettner. The fifth team member, Doug Mason, is taking the photograph.*

blanketed highlands. Reaching Atitlan, I immediately understood what so inspired Huxley. As I pedaled over brutal dirt roads that fringed its rocky shore, the lake's color mutated continuously—from subtle aquamarine to turquoise green to cobalt blue. Three active volcanoes—Toliman, Atitlan, and San Pedro—presided over the scene with majestic aloofness.

*The road to Rio Azul.*

In the ensuing years, bicycle expeditions took me around the world, through the former Soviet Union and across Africa. Nowhere, in 40,000 cycling miles, did I see a place that exceeded the Maya highland's natural beauty or human richness.

When I returned from Africa in late 1993, I noticed two issues making news: The Internet was growing at a rate of 23 percent monthly, and *Time* published a cover story entitled, "Lost Secrets of the Maya: What new discoveries tell us about their world—and ours." Inside, one paragraph read:

> *"Propelled by a series of dramatic discoveries, Mayanism has been transformed over the past thirty years from an esoteric academic discipline into one of the hottest fields of scientific inquiry today—and the pace of discovery is faster than ever."*

I was intrigued. The story recounted discoveries by a "new breed" of Mayanists. Arthur Demarest was finding evidence at Dos Pilas, Guatemala, that suggested warfare may have been the chief contributor to the collapse; Diane and Arlen Chase were finding similar proof at Caracol, Belize. Pat Culbert rather bluntly stated that, "The Maya were overpopulated and they over-exploited their environment and millions of them died." All of these factors alluded to parallels in today's world—especially at a time when tribal fratricide was destroying Bosnia, global population was doubling every twenty-seven years, and tropical rain forest in the Amazon were disappearing at a rate of one acre per minute. Despite the breakthroughs, the article concluded that the mystery of the collapse remained.

Elsewhere in the media, Mayanists such as Linda Schele, Kathryn Josserand,

David Stuart, and Nikolai Grube were attracting attention for their contributions to an "epigraphic revolution." The Maya developed the most complex pre-Columbian writing system (and one of only five in the ancient world's history). These epigraphers were "cracking the code" at the rate of a character a month or more, and in the process, filling in many of the blanks left open in the 150-year history of Maya archaeology.

Decipherment always has been a great field for amateurs. Jean-François Champollion, an unemployed history teacher, discovered the key to deciphering the Rosetta stone; architect Michael Ventris made a pivotal stride deciphering ancient Mycenaean language; and Linda Schele, who is among the greatest living epigraphers, was a studio art teacher before visiting Palenque as a tourist and becoming terminally hooked on the Maya. My idea: Use the Internet to galvanize many "amateurs" to concentrate on the collapse mystery—in effect, harness the intuitive energy of the Internet much the way architects of the Classic Maya civilization harnessed social energy to build great temples and cities.

Archaeologists like David Freidel, Skip Messenger, Arlen Chase, and Richard Leventhal bought into the idea immediately—not for its discovery potential but because it would introduce the Maya to a whole new audience. (Although they study the past, archaeologists uni-

formly share a passion for the welfare of today's six million Maya.) Our request was simple: Answer questions of an online audience and, more important, pose them, too—thus giving people from a broad swath of disciplines an opportunity to contribute to the science.

For the next eight months, I worked in tandem with Joel Halvorson at TIES, Cathy de Moll at TBT International, Jennifer Gasperini at Hamline University's Center for Global Environmental Education, Steve Buettner, and the MECC software company to build an online program and World Wide Web page (http://www.mecc.com/mayaquest.html). The Web page would offer biweekly updates, real-time photographs, teacher lesson plans, news groups, a connection to archaeologists, and a balloting mechanism wherein an online audience could help the team decide its route and how to make practical decisions during the journey's course. In short, this Internet program would relegate the cyclists to the condition of a computer icon—serving largely as conduits for a larger, more potent team of explorers. Hence, MayaQuest would unfold in parallel worlds: that of the Maya and that of cyberspace.

Would this experiment work? Or, as one fourteen-year-old computer whiz suggested, would people vote for us to eat Doritos and dog food and tell us to come home?

We chose bicycles for MayaQuest for the exact reason most North Americans avoid them—they're slow. At eight miles per hour you notice minutiae; auditory and olfactory sensations come into play. The mechanical whine of the ocependula, a trail of leaf-cutter ants, the smell of tortillas wafting from a nearby hut become part of the experience you would miss from an automobile. It's the difference between musing over a poem and speed-reading it. One allows for reflection.

MayaQuest began in Merida, Mexico, on February 1, 1995, when Doug, Steve, Julie, and I pedaled southward on custom-made mountain bikes loaded with 80 pounds of equipment apiece. Along with the necessary gear—clothes, tent, sleeping bag, etc., we also carried cameras, Trimble Global Positioning Systems (GPS), laptop computers, broadcast-quality Hi-8 video cameras, and an $18,000 Rockwell EXEC*SAT satellite dish. Nick, the logistics coordinator, piloted a Hummer all-terrain vehicle loaded with a 150-pound Kodak digital camera, bike parts, three produce boxes full of Julie's Maya books, Doug's four cameras and gear, and enough film to shoot 22,000 frames. Nick's job—to courier Atlanta-bound CNN tapes from the team's remote locations—would occupy three days weekly; the remaining time he provided team support.

In three months, the online audience sent us on a convoluted, 3,224-mile loop through the northern lowlands (Mexico's Yucatán Peninsula), the southern lowlands (Belize, northern Honduras, and northern Guatemala), and Guatemala's highlands. Each Monday, we opened our EXEC*SAT, aimed the dish at a geosynchronous IN-MARSAT satellite hovering 22,400 miles above Ecuador, and posted an update and a ballot. The following Wednesday, we posted a second update and got Monday's voting results. The online audience could send us to one of four sites, each of which had an attendant expert. The team would cycle to the destination, explore the site, interview the archaeologist, and post his or her question with the following Monday's update.

In eastern Belize, cave expert Derrick Chan, a Belizian Maya who worked as a park ranger, led us to Petroglyph Cave. We hiked over a little-used trail, through thick tropical foliage, up a steep hill, along a cliff, and finally down a huge basin perhaps a mile in diameter and half as deep. We had to use webbing from the Hummer's luggage rack, plus a rope, to lower ourselves onto a ledge from where we could climb downward into the widening depression along a spiraling trail. An hour later, the enormous hole though which we entered had diminished in size to that of a peephole, and we found ourselves beneath a rock dome. Through it a shaft of afternoon light angled through heavy humidity and suffused the cave's floor in a magical silky glow. A clear stream entered one side of the basin and exited another. In one place, rocks formed natural terraces whose edges were rounded by ancient waterfall; they produced the appearance of cascading, crystalline rock. The glyphs for which the cave is named were etched into the sides of these terraces in "stepped fret" design. Deeper down, we found 1,200-year-old ceramics on the ground, looking as if their owners would be along at any moment to pick them up.

Before we entered the cave, we posted a ballot that read:

A local guide told us today about Petroglyph Cave. Inside we'd find pottery and ancient Maya writing on the walls. He says we're supposed to get permission from the Belizian government. Ethically, we know we should, but between biking back and forth to the capital and waiting hours, perhaps days for the paperwork, we'd use up all of our free time. What should we do?

*Camp Six Trail, Belize.*

1. Go see the caves without permission.
2. Miss the caves all together.

This ballot generated more responses than any of the previous sixteen. Many people suggested that we just go, that getting permission is just a formality and that we'll hate ourselves for missing the wonders of that cave. One school wrote, "Remember teenage rule number 228: Do not ask permission; if caught, beg forgiveness."

Many more people, including most of our Maya experts, strongly advised against entering the cave without permission. They cited the fact that we'd be setting a bad example for kids and that we'd being showing a lack of respect for our host country. Others were appalled that we'd even raise the question.

But by raising the question (we did end up getting permission), we ignited a discussion and brought unprecedented attention to an important issue. At the end, John Hoopes from the University of Kansas wrote, "As an archaeologist who has dealt with looted sites for more than fifteen years, the issue of permission was particularly important to me... thank you for introducing a whole new audience to the universe of the Maya!"

Our postings made another splash a week later when we rolled into Caracol in southwestern Belize. Diane and Arlen Chase were waiting.

The Chases are not your typical archaeologists. They are a young, handsome couple with kids ages five, four, and five months. They look like the type of family you see in minivan ads, except they live in the jungle four months of every year. They stood in the doorway of a thatched-roof hut next to a sign that read: "WELCOME TO CARACOL . . . ALL THE RUMORS ARE TRUE."

The Chases have been coming to Caracol for the past eleven years. Funded mainly by the University of Central Florida, they have transformed what was once a bunch of mounds in the jungle into the most impressive Maya site in Belize. Thanks to their work, dozens of pyramids now tower above the trees, a laboratory is stacked full of artifacts, and the story we have of the ancient Maya is much richer.

The Chases believe that Caracol was once the greatest of all Maya sites, and they have the evidence to back it up. Their studies reveal that some 115,000 people once inhabited the site, that it encompassed 177 square kilometers in the year 562 A.D., and that it defeated the giant city of Tikal. Lately they have mapped an incredible maze of terraced fields throughout the site that suggests that the Maya were far more organized than previously thought. (Such agriculture requires careful urban planning and a complex bureaucracy.)

We started our weekend visit Friday afternoon when we opened our EXEC*SAT dish and established a computer link with teacher Kathy Kraemer and Como Elementary School in St. Paul, Minnesota. The students had gathered in the auditorium to watch a projected image of a com-

*Glyphs at Caracol.*

puter screen. Joel Halvorson from the TIES/InforMNs project booted up the MayaQuest Internet Center and waited with a blank screen.

Suddenly the words, "GREETINGS COMO SCHOOL FROM CARACOL, BELIZE" appeared on the auditorium wall. At our end, the Chases and the MayaQuest team sat in a jungle laboratory. Once we established the link, we typed a message that instantly appeared on Como's auditorium wall—more than 3,000 miles away!

The school sent us a packet of questions for the Chases and answers to a question we had posted a week earlier. We went off-line for an hour, typed the responses, and sent them back. We also sent a Kodak digital image of the team and the Chases standing in front of a stela. We accomplished all of this with technology that fits on the back of a bicycle.

On Saturday morning, we were on hand for a truly important discovery. On Caana ("Sky House"), Caracol's biggest structure, Arlen Chase unearthed an important text that had been buried under a platform for more than 1,300 years. A small crowd gathered as he crawled halfway into a long, flat hole. Once he reached the glyphs, he used dental picks to scrape off dirt the way a dentist would clean plaque off teeth. The glyphs began to take shape. The date appeared first and as Arlen yelled out "2 Pop. . ." Nikolai Grube, a famous epigrapher from Germany, typed the data into a computer. A program almost instantaneously translated the Maya date into one we could understand. The text recorded an event that took place on February 28, 680 A.D.

Nikolai crawled into the hole and continued the translation. His words came back muffled. He said that the text recorded a "star-shell" event, which is the

*Nikolia Grube and Alfonso Morales at Caracol.*

most devastating of defeats. It took place somewhere in Caracol. The text also revealed that the smaller site of Naranjo, forty-five miles distant, was involved with the event and that a Caracol king returned after being away for 267 days. Nikolai's first impression was that Naranjo had defeated Caracol and sent its king into exile.

"I don't buy that," Arlen shot back. Sweat was soaking through his shirt and his face glowed red. Caracol's importance is a touchy subject between Arlen and Nikolai: Nikolai does not believe that Caracol was as powerful as Tikal or Calakmul.

"It's right there," Nikolai replied motioning to the glyphs. "Just read them."

I knew that neither expert was truly angry. This type of interaction is as much a part of the discovery process as is excavating tombs.

Traditionally the archaeologists would study the find completely, catalog all of the evidence, and publish their results months or even years later. With MayaQuest serving as a conduit, though,

people around the world saw Caracol's stuccoed glyphs and heard the preliminary translation less than forty-eight hours after Arlen scraped off the dirt. Atzlan, the Mesoamerican news group, lit up with a spirited debate, and the Chases got almost instant feedback on their finding.

Not all Internet postings produced the desired effect, however. Two months into the expedition, I sent off the following update:

Update 4/12/95
Location: near Rio Dulce, Guatemala

Four times today we were stopped by military road blocks. Soldiers dressed for battle in fatigues, army boots, and bandoliers, wielded M-16 automatic rifles and demanded our passports. They questioned us, picked at our packs, and let us leave. The experience was a disagreeable one. Why do soldiers with machine guns have to stop simple travelers?

The fact is, the Guatemalan military is not a kind, gentle bunch. We passed one army base today. A huge arching sign over the entrance read, "Welcome to the Poptún Hell," Below

that, the base mascot: a Rambo knife skewering a beret-wearing skull. On the ground a motto read:

If I advance, follow me
If I hesitate, push me
If I retreat, kill me

The atrocities that the Guatemalan military committed in the 1980s are well-documented. They burned entire Maya villages, killing all the men and many women and children. They tortured journalists, priests, and anyone else suspected of helping leftist guerrillas. They burned down thousands of acres of rain forests so their enemies couldn't hide.

What most troubled me today was that almost every soldier that stopped me appeared to be a pure-blooded Maya. As they paged through my passport, I looked at them. They had the same sloping forehead and the same Roman nose—the same profile—I had seen on stelae at Tikal just last week. In this case, machine guns and army helmets replaced spears and plumed headdresses.

One theory of the Classic Maya collapse holds that the population was so abused by the elites that they revolted. The uprising drove all of the kings and nobles out of the cities and with them went their culture. Today, 87 percent of the population lives in poverty; 72 percent can't afford a minimum diet. Meanwhile, 2 percent of the population—the elites—holds 70 percent of Guatemala's farmland. It's the army that keeps these elites in power.

Things are getting better in Guatemala. Incidents of torture and death are down. The newspapers report that the military and the guerrillas are close to signing another peace accord, and many of the refugees who were driven out of Guatemala in the 1980s are coming back.

But at one point today, planes flew overhead and armed soldiers parachuted out. I pulled over and watched Maya peasants, wearing colorful huipiles, staring into the sky as fellow Mayas drifted down to earth like dandelion seeds. It was probably just practice, but it brought to mind the adage that people who don't know their history are doomed to repeat it. I hoped that the soldiers jumping out of those airplanes knew theirs.

Two days later we received an e-mail from one of our online experts (who asked to remain anonymous): "I would be willing to bet at least one Guatemalan government official has been assigned to monitor MayaQuest…beware of harsh reprisals for your last posting." Later, an archaeologist who also will go unnamed wrote, "The military certainly committed atrocities and the social scheme is certainly run by rich and for the rich. But in my opinion, the revolutionary left is equally guilty of atrocities and equally interested in getting in power so that they have a chance to exploit the poor . . . I decided some time ago that I care enough about Guatemala that I had to speak out even if my reaction is a minority one."

We faced a different kind of danger when the online audience voted for us to explore Rio Azul. Getting there requires a several day journey through Guatemala's Petén Jungle—a region notorious for bot flies (whose larvae burrow into your flesh), chiclero flies (whose bite causes flesh in the immediate area to die and rot), Africanized bees, ticks, malaria-carrying mosquitoes, marijuana growers, drug traffickers, a half-dozen varieties of poisonous snakes, and lately, a lack of water.

Juan Jose de la Hoya, a man who knows the Petén better than any man alive, graciously agreed to guide us to Rio Azul. "Just buy the food," he said cheerily, looking at me with his crystalline blue eyes. This was a generous offer; Juan Jose is a pro. He and his "El Sombrero" lodge on Lake Yaxhá cater to highbrow Europeans with a taste for fine wine, gourmet food, and exotic treks.

The road started out innocently enough. From Lake Yaxhá, two parallel tracks cut widely through the jungle, over forgiving hills and through dry riverbeds. North of the Maya site of Nakum, however, our luck reversed when the road narrowed to a foot path. Hills steepened. Gnarled roots and deep ruts littered the way. Sharp inclines portended menacing descents during which a salad of loose soil, and chest-high sticker bushes would await us at the bottom. Riding required quick reflexes and intense concentration—like a video game's more challenging levels when everything speeds up and the machine goes all out to eat your quarter.

Days were hot and humid, so much so that, as soon as we stopped, sweat glistened on our bodies, forming an adhesive film. By mid-afternoon our strength was drained and our reflexes dulled. We painfully churned out long miles, standing up to meet the hill only to find our legs had no torque. Our heads ached; the helmets seemed to weigh twenty pounds. On the rapid descents, our heads bobbed like those spring-neck puppies you see on rear dashboards. We pushed on because we had five day's supply of food and water, and at this rate, eight days of cycling. At night we camped at abandoned "chiclero" camps. Unshowered, we slept in sweaty heaps on top of our sleeping bags, coccooned in the day's dead insects, leaf shreds, stickers, dust, and insect repellent.

Time and time again, we were struck by the jungle's degradation. The Petén had loomed large in my imagination: Central America's largest tropical rain forest, an expanse bigger than New Hampshire and Vermont combined, an impenetrable wilderness of jaguars, lost cities, and Promethean trees. Often, downed trees completely clogged the trail. According to Juan Jose, 80 percent of the hardwoods have been culled. Mennonites from Belize, Petén's governor, Mexican logging pirates, and the Association of Industrial Loggers of the Petén (AIMPE) collectively extract four million trees annually. A snarl of uncharted logging trails—which increased in frequency as we neared the Mexican-Belize border—branched indistinguishably from established tracks. Worse, they were paving the way for desperate refugees from overcrowded cities to come here to coax a swidden subsistence out of thin topsoil. These peasants burn to erect huts, clear fields, and flush game. One such burn-off flanked our trail for the better half of the third day. The once pristine jungle lay blackened and smoldering, majestic ceiba and mahogany trees reduced to gnarled skeletons.

At about 2:30 P.M. on the third day, we came to a huge clearing where a wide, clean road branched to the northeast and a clogged bumping road twisted off to the west. Which was the road to Rio Azul? We stopped. Juan Jose rubbed his whiskered chin. "This is all new. It wasn't here six months ago."

From our panniers we pulled out the GPS and the U.S. State Department Operational Navigation Charts. It took several minutes to get the necessary three satellites for a read: 17°45.263'N 89°09.105'W. I ran my finger along the map. The north coordinate put us a mile or two from the Mexican border. But the west coordinate put us in Belize—illegally!

The good news was that we knew we had to go west. The bad news was that we had overshot Rio Azul by at least a half-day. We were exhausted. Our food supply had dwindled to four avocados, a box of Cerlac infant food, PowerBars, and a dozen cabbage-like tubers called "peruleros." Only fifteen gallons of water remained of the original fifty. And the Hummer was down to a quarter of a tank. In short, we had come less than halfway and used up three-quarters of our resources.

We headed west and experienced the worst road yet. Vegetation rioted. Hidden thorns punctured our tires at a rate of four

per hour. The sky darkened. Rain began to fall.

At dusk the Hummer—which moved even more slowly than the cyclists—caught up to us. Juan stepped out. "I don't like this road. It shouldn't be so bad."

"What do you mean?"

"The compass says we're going south. I don't think this is the right road." His eyes flashed a canine desperation. I think he was less concerned about dying than losing face. "It can't be, man!"

"Look, we have thirty minutes of light." I said. "I think we go until it gets dark then tomorrow morning we'll decide what to do. It does us no good to stay here."

*Steve Buettner suffers from nausea and hills, Todos Santos, Guatemala.*

We pushed on. I decided that if we didn't find Rio Azul tonight we'd turn back. When the Hummer ran out of fuel, the two strongest cyclists would take most of the water and return for help. We'd pray they'd chose the right paths.

At about nightfall, we came to a wall of vegetation. Steve, Nick, and I cut through it with machetes only to find that our trail forked yet again. Both trails were barely distinguishable. Juan jumped out. "Esto es!" he cried. "This goes to Rio

*Using the GPS on the road to Rio Azul.*

Azul," he said pointing to the northern branch. "The other one goes to the camp. In four kilometers you'll have water; it's teeming with parasites, but we can take buckets of it!" This, after three of the filthiest days of my life, was a gift from God.

An adventure distinguishes itself from a journey often by only one defining leg. It is necessarily the most difficult leg, where you push yourself beyond physical and psychological limits, where you augment

your endurance, discipline, and confidence. For us, that leg was the foray to Rio Azul. When we think back on MayaQuest, our memories will invariably settle on those five precarious days in the Petén Jungle.

Was the project a success? I'll let the numbers speak. During the 104 days, the Web page received 1.3 million hits—more than 12,000 a day. Linda Schele remarked, "In a way, MayaQuest did more to make people in the United States conscious of the Maya than all of the stuff all of the archaeologists have ever done."

What follows is a bold experiment— an attempt to fuse the essence of two journeys into one composition. From the land journey, we present a distillation of more than 22,000 images; from cyberspace, we offer eighty-five "gems" winnowed from more than 850 pages of online contributions. Together and in tandem, they comprise an attempt at a new genre and, perhaps, another chapter in the book of exploration.

DAN BUETTNER, JANUARY 1996

# ACKNOWLEDGMENTS

*The MayaQuest Interactive Expedition, by its very nature, was a collective effort of which I played only a part. The lion's share of credit for the project's success belongs to the following people:*

**The Team**
Julie Acuff
Nick Buettner
Steve Buettner
Doug Mason

**MayaQuest Headquarters**
Jennifer Crosby
Keyvan Hajiani
Jocey Hale
Ramzan Magomedov
Shelli Kae Sonstigaard
Linda Zespy

**Consultants**
Cathy de Moll *TBT International*
Jennifer Gasperini *Hamline University Center for Global Environmental Education*
Joel Halvorson *TIES/InforMNs project*

**Archaeologists in the field**
Ricardo Agurcia, Ph.D. *Copán, Honduras*
Wendy Ashmore, Ph.D. *Xunantunich, Belize*
Diane and Arlen Chase, Ph.D. *Caracol, Belize*
Anne Dowd *Calakmul, Mexico*
Anabel Ford, Ph.D. *El Pilar, Belize*
Brandon Lewis, Ph.D. *Xunantunich, Belize*
Patricia McAnany, Ph.D. *K'xob, Belize*
Alfonso Morales *Carcol, Belize*
Christopher Powell *Copán, Honduras*
David Sadat *Copán, Honduras*
Peter Schmidt, Ph.D. *Chichén Itzá, Mexico*

**Online Experts**
Ed Barnhart
George Bey III, Ph.D.
Christopher Dore, Ph.D.
Sam Edgerton, Ph.D.
David Freidel, Ph.D.
John Hoopes, Ph.D.
Linda Schele, Ph.D.
Kristiaan D. Villela
James Woods, Ph.D.

**Consulting Mayanists**
T. Patrick Culbert, Ph.D.
Elin Danian, Ph.D.
Nick Hayes, Ph.D.
Kevin Johnson, Ph.D.
Kathryn Josserand, Ph.D.
Ed Kurjack, Ph.D.
Richard Leventhal, Ph.D.
Linnea Wren, Ph.D.

**Sponsors**
3M Foundation
Huffy
MECC
Nystrom Division of Herff Jones
ProColor
Prodigy
Target Stores
WTC/Ecomaster, Inc.

**Suppliers**
3M Scotchlite
Bell Sports
Copies Now
Datotek
Eastman Kodak
Freewheel Bicycle
Hummer
InMotion
Kiss
MTI
National Camera Exchange
One Sport
Overland Equipment
Park Tool
Patagonia
PowerBars
Rockwell
Safe Reflections
Scientific Concepts
Sundog
Trend Enterprises
Trimble Navigation
Vaughn Communications
Wheely

**Educators**
Paula Burtness *Red Wing Elementary, MN*
Dan Eckberg *KHOP TV Hopkins, MN*
Kathy Kraemer *Como Elementary, MN*
Mary Mason *Gwinnet Co. Public Schools, GA*
Gayle Spinell-Gellers *Coral Springs Middle School, FL*

**Special Thanks to**
Jennifer Block and Steve Perlstein *Onion Press, Inc.*
Roger and Dolly Buettner
Juan José de la Hoya
Skip Messenger, Ph. D. *Hamline University*
Phyllis Messenger
Janice McDonald *CNN Newsroom*
Severn Sandt *ABC Prime Time Live*
Brian Woodey *Belize Department of Archaeology*

# Section One
# NORTHERN LOWLANDS

The Maya didn't have any animals that they could ride or have carry things for them. It was a reasonable arrangement to have central government preside over a rather modest territory, a couple of days' walk out from the capital. So the city-state became the standard. This is what happened even in ancient societies that did have draft animals, like the city-states of Greece or Mesopotamia (modern Iraq).

**—DAVID FREIDEL**

*The sun rises over
Chichén Itzá's
"Mercado."*

3

*El Castillo at Chichén Itzá also is known as the Temple of Kulkulcan. During equinox, shadows cast by the stepped levels of the pyramid create the illusion of a descending serpent.*

Uxmal and Chichén Itzá are referred to by scholars as "Post-Classic" sites; that is, sites that continued to flourish subsequent to the ninth century collapse of the Classic Maya civilization. But did they remain Maya to the end? Traditional scholarship has long held that both were "invaded" by cultural influences (Toltecs) from Central Mexico. Evidence is cited that the Mexican "feathered serpent" was imported and displaced older forms of Maya religions. Moreover, the Maya word "Itzá" means, "People who speak differently," thus implying foreign occupation.—**SAM EDGERTON**

The reason Linda Schele and I argue against a Toltec invasion is that while the style of art in Chichén Itzá is different from the lowland Classic period cities, the content of the images, what they mean, is clearly derived from the Maya culture rather than from Mexico.

—DAVID FREIDEL

*The Chak Mool at Chichén Itzá closely resembles sculptures in the central Mexican city of Tula.*

*Chichén Itzá's Caracol Observatory. The structure's spiral-like inner chambers inspired its name. In Spanish, "Caracol" means snail shell.*

 To make their observations of the sun, moon, and planets, Maya used the naked eye, keeping careful records in books. They used the horizon and set up their buildings to help them measure alignments. They did not do this for science, but rather to learn about the rhythms of the cosmos so that they could understand better who the gods were and how the world worked.—LINDA SCHELE

*During Spring and Autumn equinoxes, the House of the Seven Dolls' central door frames the rising sun. Dzibilchaltún.*

The Maya of the Yucatán saw war and ball game sacrifice as going together. There are few ball courts in the northern Maya lowlands dating before the Terminal Classic period (800–1000 A.D.) when the great struggles between Chichén Itzá and its enemies were going on. The Great Ball Court at Chichén Itzá is a monument to success in these wars.—**DAVID FREIDEL**

*A carving from the Great Ball Court at Chichén Itzá depicts the victor holding the defeated ballplayer's decapitated head.*

The ball-court scene shows two groups of people proceeding towards a central kneeling individual who has just had his head cut off. The man who cut his head off is standing next to him, holding the head by a long hank of hair and also holding a big stone knife. (Actually, this kind of knife was used to take out hearts; axes were used to cut off heads.)—**DAVID FREIDEL**

*Seated on a throne of human bones and holding a severed head, this Maya figurine represents the god of sacrifice.*

11

What actually collapsed in the Classic Maya collapse? All archaeologists can say for sure is that in a number of Classic sites grouped in and around the Petén region of Meso-america, hieroglyphic record carving ceased by 909 A.D.—about the same time all monumental buildings were left to squatters. What sparked this? It may have been the extraordinary appearance of Halley's comet in March–April 837 A.D. Local shamans in a number of cities may have inter-preted this apparition as a clear message of displeasure from the gods, in effect telling the people that their old votives were no longer acceptable.

—SAM EDGERTON

Stars streak across the Mexican sky at Dzibilnocac. The Maya made careful observations of the movements of the stars, planets, sun, and moon. They based their sacred calendar on these records.

*Candles illuminate
a Maya home.
Yaxuná, Mexico.*

Maya lords lived in stone houses with plaster over the walls. Farmers and villagers lived in houses made of wood and thatch. These are still used throughout the region today.—**LINDA SCHELE**

*At breakfast in the home of Yaxuná's mayor, the team gets a taste of local culture along with instant coffee and bread.*

15

Yucatec Maya are very knowledgeable about the natural environment, about the spirits and the gods of their place, and about practical things like how to build houses and organize work. —DAVID FREIDEL

*In less than half an hour, Maya men reduce a once-proud buck into four slabs of venison. The man who shot the deer offers the team the head, a delicacy, in a gesture of appreciation for helping him carry it home.*

*New traditions replace old ones: a Catholic shrine to the dead pays homage to ancestors. Fifteen hundred years ago, Maya nobles and kings traveled to the underworld in deep trance states to communicate with their ancestors.*

*The House of the Seven Dolls at Dzibilchaltún, built around 700 A.D., later was covered by a larger pyramid. In the thirteenth century, distraught priests tunneled back through to the structure to the original building and buried seven clay figurines as an offering.*

 Maya kings had the powers of shamans; they could communicate directly with the ancestors and they could talk to the gods. Shamans in villages had these powers also; the big differences lay in the instruments they could use to wield power and in the knowledge they could use to amplify power. What's the difference between a tricycle and a jet airplane? They both transport you, but one is bigger, faster, and more powerful than the other. The difference between Don Pablo's little wooden altar and the great pyramids is the same. Both allow communication with the gods and ancestors. But the pyramid worked for the benefit of a large community, while Don Pablo's altar helped a sick man.—DAVID FREIDEL

*Shaman Don Pablo arranges his altar, lighting seven candles and filling seven gourds with "balche," a fermented corn beverage. He will call upon seven gods to help exorcise "bad wind" from a patient's ear.*

Maya shamans are very good at using herbs and plants. Their medicine is different than ours. They are not as good as we are at healing the body, but they are much better at working with people who are sad, lonely, and with family problems. They concentrate on helping people fit into their families and towns better. They try to bring each individual into balance with the world.—**LINDA SCHELE**

*Don Pablo begins a healing ceremony.*

*Don Pablo displays divining crystals he uses*
*in rituals to help members of the community.*

*Having learned to discern the different ways divining crystals capture light, Shaman Don Pablo can look into the past and advise his clients on the future.*

The shaman you mentioned is similar to the medicine men of North American tribes. They also use crystals, sweet grass tobacco (which they consider sacred), and other charms to "cure." A Maya shaman going into a trance is reminiscent of the vision that the Native Americans sought, so they could garner help from the spirits.—**VAL McGRUDER**

A three-stone hearth supports a tortilla "comal." The stones represent those that the Maya gods set in the sky to center the universe. When a family sets a hearth in a new house, they replicate these events, metaphorically centering their home.

24

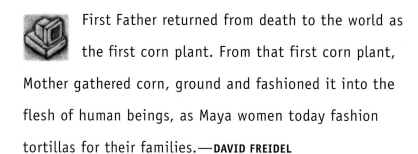 First Father returned from death to the world as the first corn plant. From that first corn plant, Mother gathered corn, ground and fashioned it into the flesh of human beings, as Maya women today fashion tortillas for their families. —**DAVID FREIDEL**

*Experienced hands mold heavy maize dough into the day's tortillas. Yaxuná, Mexico.*

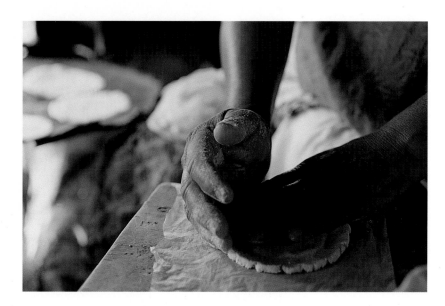

The kids you see in Yaxuná are mostly boys. Boys collect firewood for their kitchen, which means finding and chopping dry wood with steel machetes—hard going—then carrying back bundles of sticks as big as themselves. Girls, by age twelve, are helping their mothers and aunts clean, wash clothes by hand, prepare food for meals, and especially tend to the many younger children of the family.

—DAVID FREIDEL

*A boy shows off his prize turkey in Yucatán, Mexico. Just like their ancestors, Yucatec Maya still prepare a turkey stew made with peppers and served with tortillas.*

*A young boy sells bananas near Balamku, Mexico.*

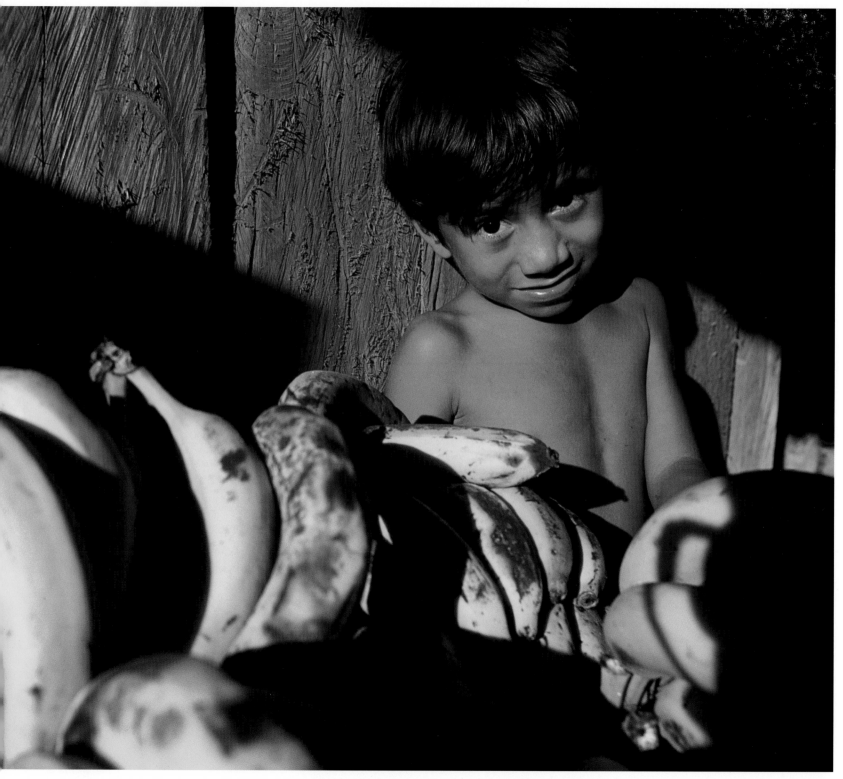

*Leaf-cutter ants, common throughout the Maya
area, can defoliate vast tracts of the land.*

*Nick cycles through Guatemala's Petén Jungle en route to Rio Azul. Twenty-four hours later, he pulled 120 ticks from his body.*

 Several years ago a student from Tulane University, where I did my graduate work, was working in Yucatán and fainted in the field from not watching the sun. He fell into an ant hill and was bitten so badly for four hours that he never recovered and died in a U.S. hospital a month later. It is serious business.

—GEORGE BEY

Europeans who colonized the New World also had the attitude that their beliefs, mores, and culture were "correct," and that the indigenous Maya and American Indian cultures were wrong and needed to be conquered and converted to Christianity. For this reason, much of the rich cultural heritage and history of these people has been lost forever.

—SCOTT FRYKMAN

*Icons of clashing cultures, Coca-Cola and Catholicism increasingly win out over traditional Maya customs.*

*The stone masonry and lattice work design on this building from Chichén Itzá shows a stylistic influence from the Puuc region, the area encompassing sites such as Uxmal, Sayil, and Kabáh.*

 A Maya building, even an ordinary house, was not only a shelter from the rain; a Maya sculpture, even an ordinary pot, was not just an innocuous something standing on the ground. These and all other Maya artifacts represented their most sophisticated technological means of communicating with and ameliorating the supernatural who might then be persuaded to grant more material prosperity to people on earth.

—SAM EDGERTON

*On this vessel, Maya artists painted the image of a long-nosed god wearing a water lily headdress.*

*In a humiliating gesture of dominance, a victorious warrior clutches the hair of a defeated foe.*

*A carved relief at Chichén Itzá shows an eagle devouring a sacrificial victim's heart. The eagle may refer to a clan of warriors who dressed as eagles in battle.*

For all the unusual symbolic ideas that the Maya manage to communicate through their art and writing systems, many themes emerge that are common to other cultures throughout the ages. Warfare internecine competition from power, concern with agricultural fertility, with death or sacrifice, are just a few. —**ANNE DOWD**

*A jaguar devours a human heart, ripped from the chest of a sacrificial victim. This relief found at Chichén Itzá may refer to a fierce clan of warriors who dressed as jaguars in battle.*

Were the Maya beginning to lose faith in their gods (and their divine kings, the gods' surrogates on earth) between 800–900 A.D.? Did they believe their grand temples and inscribed monuments were no longer effective in bringing about divine intercession to solve their problems? An interesting parallel might be the Roman Empire around 200–300 A.D., as the traditional Greek-based religion began to lose its potency in favor of new spiritual notions (Christianity) coming from the east. Art styles of Rome began to change. Monuments like the Arch of Constantine suddenly reflected new oriental influences, replacing many older classical forms. Isn't this something like the stylistic transition we also observe in Post-Classic Maya sites like Chichén Itzá?

—SAM EDGERTON

*Feathered serpents in
Chichén Itzá's art
bear resemblance to
Quetzalcóatl, a god in
the central Mexican
pantheon.*

The Yucatán area was and continues to be a hurricane-prone region. Looking back over the last century, I counted no fewer than 100 tropical storms or hurricanes that have affected the Yucatán by either passing directly across parts or all of it . . . I suspect that any people living there for any length of time would most likely come to deal with these storms as seasonal events and only in such cases where the same area was hit again and again in a short period would you expect culture-wide distress. This is not to say this has never occurred, as south Florida was assaulted by seven hurricanes within a five-year period in the 1940s. Many people did leave the area, never to return, and the economy suffered accordingly. —DAN GORE, ENGINEER AND METEOROLOGICAL STUDENT

*View from the steps of the House of the Governor. Uxmal, Mexico.*

*Stone warriors guard the back of the*
*Codz Poop at Kabáh, Mexico.*

I do not think that earthquakes caused the collapse of the Maya civilization. Earthquakes may have affected a few Maya sites but not the entire civilization. I am skeptical because the majority of sites on the Yucatán Peninsula are in a seismically quies-cent region. Even large earthquakes in the seismic zones cause only relatively mild shaking in the Yucatán.

—MARK GORDON, POST-DOCTORAL SCIENTIST

*Late afternoon sunlight bathes the Palace at Sayil, Mexico.*

*A testimonial to the king's mastery at harnessing social energy, "El Castillo" towers above Chichén Itzá. The ancient Maya used neither beasts of burden nor the wheel to build their temples.*

# SOUTHERN LOWLANDS

The team moved across once-ancient frontier in Maya country, from the plains of the northern lowlands into the rolling hill country of the southern lowlands. The frontier runs roughly along the line of 18 degrees north latitude. The pioneering farmers who settled Maya country 3,000 years ago all had a great deal in common, but over the centuries the northern and southern Maya communities gradually became distinct. In the southern lowlands, governments regularly started using public carved texts in glyphs to declare policy and royal power by the second century A.D. In the northern lowlands, the rulers only rarely used writing on public monuments in the Classic period. Indeed, for many Maya scholars, the northern lowlands were only marginal participants in the fluorescence of the Classic civilization.

—**DAVID FREIDEL**

*The temples of Tikal penetrate the canopy of the Petén Jungle. Tikal, a powerful city-state, once dominated many cities in the Maya lowlands. Vying for power with Calakmul, the two cities created warring alliances.*

*Originally discovered in 1912 by a Harvard University research team, Río Bec B was subsequently lost for sixty until film-makers rediscovered the site in 1973.*

*A rubber tapper's footpath doubles as a mountain bike trail for the MayaQuest team. Petén, Guatemala.*

Rebuilt three times
by divine kings,
the ball court lay at
the heart of Copán's
ceremonial center.

 The ancient Maya game was played with a solid rubber ball about the size of a bowling ball and as lively as a superball. It hurt when it hit bare skin, so the players wore padding of leather and cotton to protect themselves.—**DAVID FREIDEL**

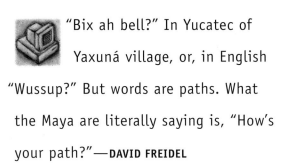"Bix ah bell?" In Yucatec of Yaxuná village, or, in English "Wussup?" But words are paths. What the Maya are literally saying is, "How's your path?"—**DAVID FREIDEL**

*Cave's Branch, Belize.*

Maya artists created mosaic masks like this one, inlaying chips of jade, coral, and shell.

The stucco facade of El Castillo at Xunantunich shows "Pax" monsters oozing a sacred substance from their mouths.

 The Maya, from the beginning of their civilization, fought wars between rival states. The prospect of war likely encouraged the elite to create many occasions for diplomatic reinforcement of friendly ties. Gift-giving, banquets, state visits, and trade pacts were certainly established practices of the ancient Maya. Ironically then, warfare among the Maya throughout most of the civilization's history did not cause massive chaos and poverty, but rather spurred the production of beautiful and expensive crafts and magnificent public plazas and buildings, designed to reinforce the alliances between states.

—DAVID FREIDEL

*A victorious Bonampak lord towers over a conquered enemy. The lord sports the rich regalia of warfare. The skull of a previous victim hangs around his neck, proclaiming his prowess in battle.*

The idea that the Maya needed extraterrestrials to make their buildings and tools insults the creative genius of Native Americans. —**LINDA SCHELE**

*The temples of Tikal: Manpower alone raised these monumental stone buildings from the ground.*

*A product of years of building, Palenque's Palace is a maze of structures that once was the center of court life, housing the royal family and creating a backdrop for ritual.*

 Maya centers had many purposes, including government business, economic exchange, and military organization. In today's world, we separate sacred places from other kinds of places a bit differently than the ancient Maya did. For the Maya, carrying out government business in the "Sky Throne" palace, or right next to it, was okay. If you think about Washington, D.C., and the magnificent temples that we have created for revered leaders there, or the wonderful pictures and sculptures that decorate our Capitol building, the combination of sacred spaces and political spaces is not such a strange idea for us.—**DAVID FREIDEL**

A worker takes a break deep in the core of Copan's Structure 16. A honey-comb of tunnels have enabled archaeologists to explore earlier construction phases of this temple. Maya kings typically destroyed the facades of their predecesors' structures, using the cut stone for their own temples.

 Most Maya pyramids were built with a rubble core of some sort. This core would be covered with cut stone, usually limestone. In most cases this limestone would in turn be covered with stucco. However, the Maya typically built pyramids on top of earlier ones.—GEORGE BEY

The work of archaeologist Simon Martin is revealing that Calakmul, in particular, was quite active in marrying off its daughters to allied sites. Calakmul women who intermarried into other sites were an essential part of the successful strategy that led to the defeat of Tikal. As epigraphy develops, especially in the area of identifying place names from within sites, I believe we will find more evidence of women playing a large role in the forging of alliances between sites.—ED BARNHART

*One of the largest buildings in the Maya realm, Structure I at Calakmul towers over the treetops.*

In its heyday, the city of Palenque must have looked like it was floating across Creation Mountain. The main buildings of the center and the magnificent palaces of the most responsible families in the government clustered on a long, wide terrace in the middle of a wall of mountains. Before the mountain wall stretched the rolling hills and hazy plains of the gulf coast of Mexico. The palaces and temples were brightly painted red and had many other colors, blue, gold, black, and cream in the stucco sculpture panels on their roofs and walls. These are among the most graceful buildings ever imagined by Maya master builders, and they must have stood out against the green flowering orchards and shade trees on the terraces of the city surrounding them.—DAVID FREIDEL

*Palenque at sunrise.*

 Palenque was, I believe, allied with the royal house of Tikal against the Calakmul kings and their vassals. Among the supporters of Calakmul were the kings of Yaxchilán and Piedras Negras. These cities commanded the Usumacinta River, but Palenque commanded the route west to Mexico's vast interior.—**DAVID FREIDEL**

*Palenque's kings record a victorious battle by depicting an elite captive awaiting sacrifice.*

The Usumacita River serves as a highway of commerce for the Maya of
Yaxchilan and Piedras Negras. Steve Buettner and the rest of the
MayaQuest team used the river to travel from Guatemla to Mexico.

 Caracol commanded the trade routes from other kingdoms in the interior to the coast, with its rich canoe trade. (It's a lot cheaper to move cotton, salt, chocolate, stone tools, and maize by canoe than by person-power—no draft animals here in antiquity!)—**DAVID FREIDEL**

The reason the Maya at Caracol changed burial practices might be that the religion changed. Perhaps the sun played an important part in the earlier religion, but not in the later version. And maybe the stress of changing from the old religion to the new one was so great that it caused the civilization to fall.

—M. DERRICK

*Sunset from Caana, Caracol.*

The fingers found in the bowls could be those of slaves. Because fingers are the part of the body used most in manual labor, the fingers of slaves were probably placed near the burial area so the slaves could continue to serve the buried person in the afterlife.—YUAN, A TEN-YEAR-OLD MAYAQUEST PARTICIPANT

*A "finger bowl" from a burial at Caracol.*
*Perhaps a sign of homage, elites were often*
*buried with caches of human fingers.*

Archaeologists usually find ancient garbage, and by the time an artifact is ready to be taken away, it is usually worn and broken—not the thing that most museum visitors want to see.—**CHRISTOPHER DORE**

*A Guatemalan worker in Topoxte clears dirt from remnants of ancient incensarios once used to burn sacred copal incense.*

A "chultun"—or
ancient storage cellar
—that once may have
held corn or ramon
nuts now serves as
a bin for discarded
potsherds. Calakmul,
Mexico.

*Archaeologist Christopher Powell carefully brushes dirt from a 1,400-year-old skeleton in Copán, Honduras. Working many tedious hours, he used a dental pick to pull dirt away from the preserved mat the dead warrior rests upon.*

*A tibia and femur excavated at Topoxte, Guatemala.*

 Archaeology is a field science, so we get only one chance to do the work right—the first time. We destroy the patterns as we excavate them and can only restore them from our notes, the artifacts, and the many scientific tests we can do to study the materials.—**DAVID FREIDEL**

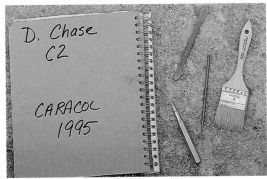

*Diane Chase keeps a notebook to record the progress of each "operation" during the spring season at Caracol.*

An archaeology student labels pottery sherds with numbers recording the exact location where they were found.

 When you read an archaeologist's theory about a past civilization in a newspaper, magazine, or on TV, don't necessarily take what they say as the "truth."

—CHRISTOPHER DORE

Professional archaeologists go to extreme lengths to be careful with archaeological remains. We pride ourselves on the fact that the painstaking methods and patience of our practitioners are legendary. Our ability to work in foreign countries, handle incredibly rare and valuable objects, and deal with ancient and delicate materials is possible because we are—as a rule—honest, responsible, and mature in the way we practice science.

—JOHN HOOPES

*A page from an archaeologist's
journal working at Caracol, Belize.*

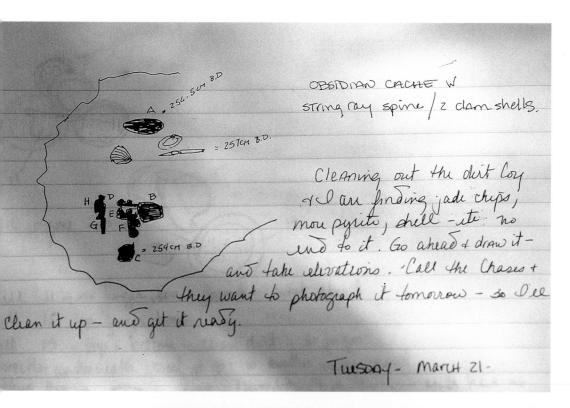

OBSIDIAN CACHE w
string ray spine / 2 clam shells.

Cleaning out the dirt coy
+ I am finding jade chips,
more pyrite, shell - etc. no
end to it. Go ahead + draw it -
and take elevations. Call the Chases +
they want to photograph it tomorrow - so I'll
clean it up - and get it ready.

Tuesday - March 21.

 Textbooks usually just try to introduce a subject without getting into the disagreements too deeply. For this reason, textbooks usually talk about the things that most experts agree on and have settled during years of discussion, investigation, and analysis. But the exciting real world of science is a place full of disagreements and competing ways of observing and understanding nature. —**DAVID FREIDEL**

*Nikolai Grube shines a flashlight on a newly discovered capstone to
illuminate the carving of an elite lord dressed in ritual regalia.
Archaeologists Arlen and Diane Chase discuss the significance of the
monument with their students.*

 The prehistoric Maya were lovers of color. Paints came from plants, minerals, and perhaps insects. There were reds and oranges, tan, pink, yellow, brown, blue, black, and white. Basic colors were not usually mixed to form additional colored paint. Instead, thin coats of different colored paint were applied over each other. The process gave the visual illusion of color mixing.

—CHRISTOPHER DORE

*A Lacandón Maya admires the murals of Bonampak, painted more than one thousand years ago by his ancestors. Maya artists used attapulgite clay to achieve the rich blue color in the murals. Today we use this substance in our carbonless copies.*

*Maya in shape, this vessel from Tikal shows the influence of Teotihuacán, which lies near what is today Mexico City. This foreign city was influential in Maya culture, bringing a new, more lethal, style of warfare to the region during the Early Classic Period.*

*Music fit for a king:
A carved jade
flute from Tikal.*

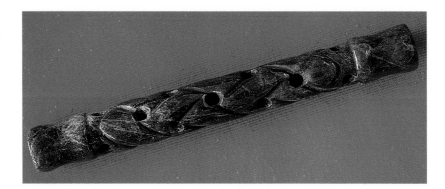

We know from murals, archaeological excavation, and painted ceramics that the Maya composed and played music, with drums and flutes and shell trumpets and rattles. The Maya enjoyed putting on complex religious and social cere-monies that included dancing and masked actors.—**GEORGE BEY**

*The murals of Bonampak depict a procession of musicians shaking gourd rattles.*

*Recorded for eternity,
a ruler from Arroyo
de Piedras is clad in
regal costume.*

*A lintel from Yaxchilán records the controversial accession of ruler Bird Jaguar. The son of a woman from Calakmul, he was chosen as heir to the throne over the sons of a Yaxchilán noble woman. A conflict in the royal house ensued.*

Was most Maya art really "art," or was it more like the murals and monuments to Mao, Lenin, and Saddam Hussein? Some people feel that propagandistic art is the antithesis of true art, which is done "for art's sake" rather than in service of governmental or religious ideology —which is how most Maya art worked.—**JOHN HOOPES**

*Mounted on the wall, Palenque's Oval Palace Tablet commemorated the accession of the great king Pakal. Succeeding rulers received their crowns sitting on a throne once situated below the tablet.*

We recently learned that royal women were keepers of the holy books. This means women also were literate and could read and keep codices. Women also held office and, rarely, they became rulers. Their most powerful positions came from marriages that helped to forge alliances between different lineages. They also educated and controlled their heirs.—**LINDA SCHELE**

*A building from the North Group at Palenque. Maya architects developed a unique construction style that created a bright, spacious feeling inside buildings.*

*Lady Zak Kuk of Palenque passes the crown to her son Pakal during his accession rite on July 29, 615 A.D. Lady Zak Kuk, one of two women to govern Palenque, ruled for three years before crowning her son.*

*A stone tool
found in excavations
at K'axob, Belize.*

We have discovered that, if used correctly, stone tools are very effective to cut and shape limestone for building blocks, and they are equally efficient in carving intricate designs into limestone for the carving of stelae or decorative elements on buildings. Our most recent experiments have shown us that one quarry worker can cut and trim a single 800-pound block (about 1 x .5 x .5 meter) in four days.—**JAMES WOODS**

*A worker cuts a stone to be used in consolidating a pyramid at Xunantunich, Belize.*

Maya children would have looked very strange to most of us. As infants, their heads were bound with cloth wrapped tightly across their foreheads. This did not hurt them, but as they grew it caused their heads to take on a distinctive shape. The foreheads became flat and sloped steeply backward. The backs of their heads became narrow and almost conical. They may have looked like "Coneheads" to us, but we—with our vertical foreheads—would have looked like Frankenstein's monster to them!

—JOHN HOOPES

*A royal profile:*
*A stela at Arroyo de*
*Piedras, Guatemala.*

*In this scene from the murals of Bonampak, three royal ladies perform tongue perforation, the most sacred type of bloodletting for women. Below, a woman holds Bonampak's heir as he prepares for his first bloodletting ceremony.*

*A sculpture fragment from Uxmal's Nunnery Quadrangle shows a lord displaying the gruesome marks of penis perforation. Blood spilled from the genitals represented the most precious gift a male could offer the gods.*

In a coming-of-age ceremony, young boys—perhaps twelve or thirteen—had their penises perforated for the first time. An adult male, who was the boy's guardian, cut through the top of the penis three times. After the cuts were made, the guardian put bone awls through them. Apparently adult males all wore these scars and reopened them in rituals throughout their lives.—**LINDA SCHELE**

*Blood drips from the fingers of a captured warrior in the murals at Bonampak. Captured in battle, the victorious warriors have ripped his fingernails out in an excruciating ritual of humiliation.*

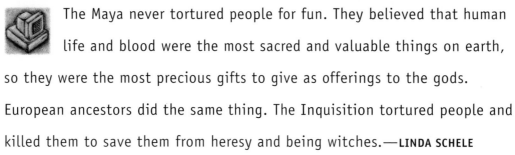 The Maya never tortured people for fun. They believed that human life and blood were the most sacred and valuable things on earth, so they were the most precious gifts to give as offerings to the gods. European ancestors did the same thing. The Inquisition tortured people and killed them to save them from heresy and being witches.—**LINDA SCHELE**

The Maya used ultra-sharp obsidian knives for bloodletting. Opthomologists still use obsidian blades for eye surgery.

A Maya glyph for "scattering" may refer to scattering droplets of blood during ritual bloodletting.

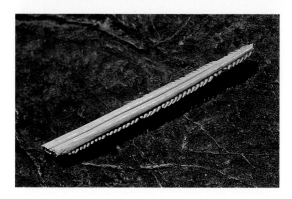

The Maya used sting ray spines, imported from the coast, to pierce various parts of their bodies in bloodletting rituals.

War and peace, destruction and prosperity, are conditions found in all civilizations, ancient and modern. It is the challenge of people in civilizations to seek ways to prevent the violence through social justice and defense of peace. But the ambitions of rulers to win victories, to command through force, to seek the easy, violent way to their goals, are a common problem in civilizations.—**DAVID FREIDEL**

*At a roadside stand in Chiapas, Dan chats with
a group of Mexican soldiers.*

*Ancient warriors battle over territory, trade routes, and power—issues common in modern day Mexico.*

*Tikal's temples jut out of the canopy of the Petén Jungle. From here, Tikal's kings once surveyed the fifty-square-mile expanse of land their city-state encompassed.*

Because I think warfare was a factor throughout Maya history, it is not easy to say that it caused the collapse as such. It must have been rather something about the way that governments fought wars, the rules of engagement, and the consequences of defeat that changed in the Late Classic Period to cause Maya governments to fight each other into a state of chaos and anarchy. One interpretation of Maya texts proposes that the Late Classic Maya had two great alliances of kings; one ruled out of Tikal and the other out of Calakmul. These alliances fought each other for supremacy for centuries, each attempting to establish a final victorious empire. In the end they destroyed themselves.—**DAVID FREIDEL**

Family disputes and intensive warfare with other sites led refugees from the royal family of Tikal to establish the splinter polity of Dos Pilas during the seventh century. Both cities claimed the Tikal emblem glyph as their own. Here the glyph is recorded on a stela from Dos Pilas.

A bone from the burial of Hasaw-Kan-K'awil, who acceded to the throne of Tikal on May 6, 682 A.D., records the capture of an elite lord from Calakmul.

*Shell rings that once adorned a headdress and jade earflares identify this
burial as that of a Tlaloc warrior. Sacrificed as part of the dedication rites
for a new building, he traveled to the underworld in bejeweled splendor.*

*Archaeologist Christopher Powell's drawing of an elite warrior's burial at Copán.*

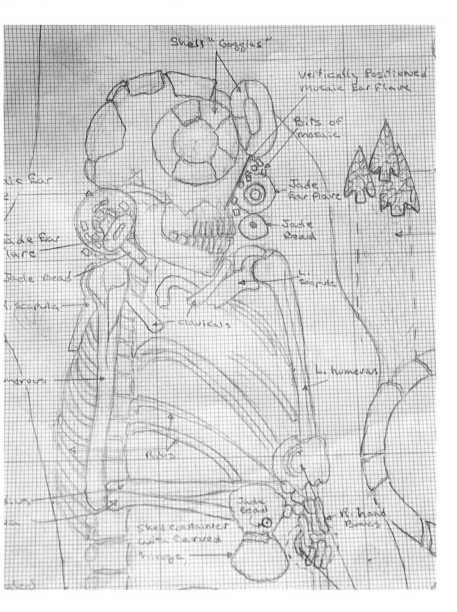

In my experience, the modern Maya do not have the same relationship with the past as do the people of many Native American nations from North America. The Maya of the Puuc region are intellectually aware that ruins and artifacts are the remains of their ancestors, but they are not emotionally attached to this past. The modern Maya that I have worked with on archaeological projects do not have the same concerns about excavating human burials that many North Americans of indigenous descent have. Death is something that many of us in North America tend to hide. We avoid the topic. This isn't the case with the Maya I know.—CHRISTOPHER DORE

# On Maya Writing

Individual glyph blocks consist of syllables that combine to make whole words, symbols that mean whole words or combinations of both. The epigrapher's task is to discern which signs are which and what they mean in context. The ancient Maya scribes were masters of variation, and almost every sign in their writing could be written a number of ways.—ED BARNHART

*All glyphic, this monument from Dos Pilas was fashioned from a creamy stone vaguely reminiscent of the marble sculptures of Greece and Rome.*

In 1952, Yuri Knorosov published a paper in a major Soviet magazine. He showed that in the Dresden Codex (one of four surviving ancient Maya books), glyphs appearing above depictions of certain animals spelled out their names in Yucatec Maya. Unfortunately, the 1950s political situation between Russia and the United States was tense and Knorosov's work was largely disregarded by the West. Critics called it communist propaganda and poor scholarship. It was not until the 1970s that Knorosov's ideas were picked up again and the real translation explosion began.
—ED BARNHART

For many years, the Maya hieroglyphic writing system was thought to record only the cycles of time. In 1960, Tatiana Proskouriakoff published clear evidence that glyphs recorded historical information. Building on this theory and on Knorosov's work proving that the glyphs reflected modern Maya languages, Floyd Lounsbury (a scholar of Egyptian hieroglyphics) proposed that if the glyphs reflected a spoken language, it must have syntax—a set word order. For example, what in English would be "Jack hit the Ball" would be "hit the ball, Jack" in Mayan. In 1973, Linda Schele and Peter Mathews tested that idea out, and in a single afternoon, deciphered most of the history of four consecutive Palenque kings!—ED BARNHART

Maya archaeology recently has changed from studying a prehistoric archaeological record to an historic one. The Maya archaeological record itself has not changed, but the advances made by epigraphers [glyph decipherers] during the last two decades now have made textual accounts a viable data source. Unfortunately, many archaeologists have been overly enthusiastic about this new data source and have accommodated, or at least de-emphasized, the archaeological data to fit the textual records.—CHRISTOPHER DORE

Maya text was used, especially by politicians, as a propaganda tool....Think about the inscriptions that are present on the many monuments in Washington, D.C. Their inscriptions talk about democracy and liberty, which are fundamental concepts of the "official ideology." These textual accounts, however, don't tell us the fact that most real political decisions are made by the economic elite, or that millions of U.S. citizens live in poverty, or that racism is a major societal problem. Why should we think that the textual accounts provided by the Maya give us any truer picture of their society and culture?—**JOHN HOOPES**

The Maya tell us to the day when events happened, and sometimes we know whether it happened during the day or night. That does not mean that Maya history was objective and true. Like our own history, it had political purposes and personal bias.—**LINDA SCHELE**

The Maya, in order to keep track of time and to communicate with a large number of people, developed a standard and complex writing system. They were able to

*The long count, one of two calendars the Maya used, records the number of days since the creation of the world on August 13, 3114 B.C. This glyph, from a stela at Dos Pilas, records the months in that count. The three bars signify the number fifteen.*

advance as a civilization because their agricultural system enabled them to feed a large number of people and to develop complete societal roles. To maintain order, they needed to communicate.—**MRS. JENKINS' 6TH GRADE CLASS, HIGHLAND VIEW MIDDLE SCHOOL, CORVALLIS, OREGON**

The surviving monuments with glyphs were like propaganda for the rulers. They told of deeds of the upper class. Sir Eric Thompson believed that glyphs were "not for the masses but restricted to members of nobility." Gaspar Antonio Chi, Diego de Landa, and Bartolome de las Casas told that historical stories often were sung and recited orally. If that is true, then everyone could know his or her history without needing to read. Thompson also said that he believed there were semiliterate people in Maya society. Maybe the farmers, women, and unskilled laborers might recognize a site's emblem glyph or certain inscriptions. So, we decided that the elites could read and write. In various degrees, other Maya could understand important glyphs or at least know their oral history. —**MRS. JENKINS' 6TH GRADE CLASS, HIGHLAND VIEW MIDDLE SCHOOL, CORVALLIS, OREGON**

*Another tree falls in the Petén: Don Jose de la Hoz clears a path.*

*Illegally cut trees litter the northern region of the Petén Jungle. The team biked on trails left by Belizian trespassers who cross the border to cut the jungle's hardwoods.*

 There is no doubt that the Petén is being abused now. Rampant overcutting of the forest is destroying the agricultural potential of delicate soils. People are not using the painstaking techniques of the ancient Maya. It would be a big mistake to think that because the ancient Maya collapsed, they didn't know how to survive in that tropical forest, and so why should we pay attention to what they did? The Maya lived and prospered in Petén between 1000 B.C. and 900 A.D. They supported millions of people and exported enough to make their royal tombs and palaces among the most sumptuous in Mesoamerica. We can learn from their successes as well as their mistakes.—DAVID FREIDEL

*Swidden, or slash-and-burn agriculture, levels a tract of forest.*

Everything was suspended animation. Everything was calm, in silence. Nothing moved, and the great expanse of the sky was empty.—**THE POPOL VUH ON THE EARTH'S BEGINNINGS, AS TRANSLATED FROM THE POPOL VUH BY PETER KNOPF'S SPANISH CLASSES, RICHWOOD HIGH, PEORIA, ILLINOIS**

*Sunset over Lake Yaxhá, Guatemala.*

*Section Three*

# HIGHLANDS

The southern Maya area must have been battered by seismic, volcanic, and land-stability processes, all three of which can combine to hammer a community. Two major plate boundaries (in the plate tectonic paradigm) are coincident with the mountainous regions—that of the Caribbean and Cocos plates for the Pacific highlands, and the Caribbean and North America plate for the Montagua drainage system. These plate boundaries are traced by the thickened crust and arc volcanic edifices that construct the mountain regions of the Maya world.—**DAVID SCHOLL, UNITED STATES GEOLOGICAL SURVEY**

*A highway snakes through Guatemala's highlands near Huehuetenago.*

Europeans seemed to know who the Maya were and wanted to gather the riches for themselves. If they had recognized and appreciated the natives as equals, they would have learned from them, and perhaps we would have, too. One can't see others as equals while killing them, their cultures, and taking their wealth. No wonder an appreciation of the Maya didn't develop in our culture. It makes me want to examine our country's dealings with other cultures today.—**MARCIA CANTRELL**

*Doug Mason and a young Mam farmer.*
*Todos Santos, Guatemala.*

Maya languages are not dialects but true languages, like Spanish and English. There are about thirty-five documented Maya languages, of which twenty-five are still spoken. Some of them are in danger of extinction, but several are spoken by hundreds and thousands of people.—**LINDA SCHELE**

*Maya traditions
endure in the highland
Guatemala town of
Todos Santos.*

*All ages participate in the Holy Week processions in Antigua, Guatemala.*

 The Maya had a calendar as complex as the Hindu calendar. They had great festivals then and continue to have them today— although most festivals today are timed by the Catholic calendar. The festivals were very complex and often involved the entire community.

—**LINDA SCHELE**

*A cross fashioned from flowers, grasses, and vegetables, awaits imminent destruction by the Holy Week processions.*

*A Cakchiquel woman (opposite)*
*in San Lucas Tolimán, Guatemala.*

*Escaping the harsh*
*afternoon sun, a man*
*in Todos Santos,*
*Guatemala, takes*
*refuge under the wide*
*brim of his hat.*

*A Mam farmer in Todos Santos, Guatemala.*

They were gifted with intelligence, they had understanding beyond their visual sight. They saw and knew everything there was in the world. Wherever they looked, in heaven and on Earth, in an instant, they understood.—**POPOL VUH ON THE CREATION OF MAN AS TRANSLATED BY PETER KNOPF'S SPANISH CLASSES, RICHWOOD HIGH, PEORIA, ILLINOIS**

*A mother and daughter shy away from the camera. Huehuetenango, Guatemala.*

 The women were created with great care by the Creator himself. While the men slept, their beautiful women came to them in their dreams. When the men awoke, their women were beside them, filling men's hearts with happiness.

**—POPOL VUH ON WOMEN AS TRANSLATED BY PETER KNOPF'S SPANISH CLASSES, RICHWOOD HIGH, PEORIA, ILLINOIS**

*A Santiago Atitlan woman transports lilies in the Highland town of San Lucas Tolimán.*

*An elite captive, exhibiting a classic Maya profile, decorates a courtyard in the Palace of Palenque.*

There is an image of the classic Maya face, which is still found in Central America. This is a handsome visage with a long Roman nose and slanting forehead and a strong chin. The ancient Maya apparently saw this as a standard of beauty and would flatten the foreheads of their offspring so that they would have a single continuous line from the tip of the nose to the top of the forehead. This was an attempt to achieve this standard, like a form of plastic surgery would be today.—**GEORGE BEY**

*A Maya farmer in Todos Santos, Guatemala.*

*A Maya musician in Todos Santos, Guatemala. Music was an important part of daily life in ancient times, as it is in modern times.*

 The animals taught the men which foods were edible. Then Ixmucan, by grinding the yellow and white ears of corn, made nine drinks from which man drew the strength of life and built up his musculature and vigor.—**POPOL VUH ON THE CREATION OF MAN AS TRANSLATED BY PETER KNOPF'S SPANISH CLASSES, RICHWOOD HIGH, PEORIA, ILLINOIS**

When a Maya farmer prepares his field, he shapes like a sculptor, like an artist, the land into the squares and rectangles that are the human design on the world. In Yucatec Maya, the word for cornfield, *Nal*, is the same as the word for a human-occupied place.—**DAVID FREIDEL**

*Maya farmer holding corn. Todos Santos, Guatemala.*

Fields are still laid out in a traditional manner near Huehuetenango, Guatemala. Long cords are stretched and folded to determine the boundaries, replicating the actions of the gods.

*A communal farm. Panajachel, Guatemala.*

 Among other things, the Maya and their neighbors invented chocolate and vanilla. Other foods discovered by the Mesoamericans include corn, tomatoes, avocados, cashews, chili peppers, pumpkins, and sweet potatoes. Chicle, the main ingredient in chewing gum, also comes from where the Maya lived. They also discovered and made the first ball.

—JOHN HOOPES

*A Cakchiquel family in San Lucas Tolimán prepares a traditional meal.*

*Maize, still a staple for the modern Maya,*
*typically is eaten in various forms at every meal.*

Maya farmers live the cycles of their plants. Maize, the great staple, requires human beings to reproduce; corn can't survive on its own anymore. It must be planted in the earth. Maya people can't survive without corn, it is their flesh. So at the center of everything important, there are people and there are plants. Food plants are not just good to eat. They are also good to think about, as symbols or metaphors for what life is really all about.—DAVID FREIDEL

*A Maya farmer in Todos Santos seeds his milpa.*

Maya curers, like Don Pablo de la Cruz as described by Dan at Yaxuná, sacrifice chickens to offer substitutes for disease to the spirits. Sacrifice is a central idea to several of our religions as well as to theirs. For me, sacrifice is about the responsibility people have to give to the world as well as to receive from it.

—DAVID FREIDEL

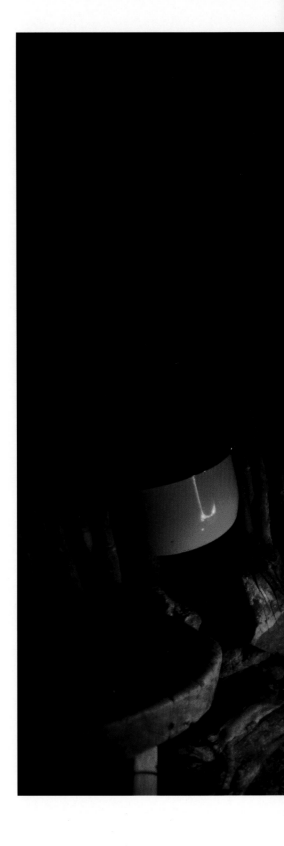

*During a healing ceremony, a Maya woman
prepares a sacrificial chicken.*

As with all people in the history of the world, the Maya were great in many things they did, but they believed in things we find hard to understand. It is important that our history does not make our ancestors heroes and saviors and their ancestors barbarians and crazy. This is the beginning of tolerance and realizing that the value of all people of the world is that they have contributed to the heritage of human beings.—LINDA SCHELE

*Decorated for Holy Week, a church in
Chichincastenango, Guatemala, displays a unique
mix of Catholicism and traditional Maya symbols.*

The mystery of the collapse, fascinating as it is, is no match for the miracle of the living Maya—graceful, intelligent people who have endured five centuries of conquest with their souls intact. They are under severe pressure today and they could use our concern, awareness, and help. They also have understandings to share with us, people to people.

—**DAVID FREIDEL**

*Modern Maya children hold candles during a Good Friday procession in Antigua, Guatemala.*

*Tikal, once a formidable super-power, now stands abandoned, inhabited only by tourists, guards, and a few archaeologists. As such, the ancient city is a reminder to us that great civilizations often sow the seeds of their own destruction.*

 All societies rise and fall. Someday, ours will, too—it's inevitable. Even though the Maya society did collapse without telling us why, look what they left behind. If their ruins reveal nothing else, it's that whatever they did do right or wrong, they did it with panache and style! So let's hope that when our turn finally comes, we, too, go out like the Maya, with an artistic bang, and not, as we seem, with only a "Warhol whimper!"—**SAM EDGERTON**

# Kids on the Collapse

I feel that Maya technology could not keep up with population growth. The Maya had many problems and only some skills. No society can stay together without more and more technology.—**WALI OSBORNE**

The people took too much from the land and didn't put anything back into it.—**BRIKTI HODGE**

I think they decided to leave everything because they wanted a simpler, easier lifestyle.—**FATIMA VILLASENOR**

People move every day from their houses because they are sick of them. They also move for health and money reasons. People are forced off their land by highways coming through or because they don't pay their bills. The Maya could have left their cities for any of these reasons.

—**RYAN HOAG, WASHBURN HIGH SCHOOL, MINNEAPOLIS, MINNESOTA**

Amid their final struggles, the Maya also may have suffered some kind of a spiritual/leadership crisis. The elites and priests could not deliver or were less able to coerce the masses to follow their lead. The population may have become disenchanted with the spiritual leadership and something like a "dark reformation" could have taken place. Consequently the cities and spiritual centers were abandoned.—**JONATHAN MOEUKE, RED WING, MINNESOTA**

Perhaps contamination of the algae they farmed (spirulina or chlorella) was the cause of the Maya demise.

—**MRS. BLACKMORE'S SPANISH CLASS, SOUTH AMBOY, NEW YORK**

I believe the Maya may have been dealt a halting blow from a virus such as Ebola. A virus could spring from over-development of a tropical area, as the Maya may have been doing while overfarming their surrounding. Moving quickly as this virus does, it would have destroyed the population and left the illusion of sudden collapse.—**MATT CONNOLLY**

*American school children follow MayaQuest via the Internet.*

*he wisdom of the ancient Maya is the wisdom of humanity. It is the wisdom of any civilization that is able to create a world out of the natural environment and sustain itself one of a large, diverse population that maintains the food supply, works together, builds together, and gets along."*

WENDY ASHMORE

MayaQuest underwent a sea change one balmy afternoon in Belize. The team stood on Xunantunich's tallest temple, El Castillo, talking with archaeologist Wendy Ashmore, looking out over the site's oddly asymmetrical lay and the Mopan river valley. We had spent two months in a quest to better understand the ancient Maya collapse. Archaeologists we met had offered explanations of environmental degradation, warfare, drought, and even volcanic eruptions. Now things began to blur: Wendy was telling us that she and her co-director, Richard Leventhal, had found evidence showing that the Maya had flourished at Xunantunich into the eleventh century; that perhaps there wasn't a collapse but a transition, that it would be more useful for us to focus on the accomplishments of the Maya than their demise.

We had chosen the collapse as the central object of MayaQuest because it offers a mirror to look at our own society. The ancient Maya, like America today, was the greatest civilization of its time and the parallels are unavoidable. As archaeologist John Hoopes put it, "The more we study the Maya, the more we consider what really matters to us. Looking at their demise forces us to contemplate the process of cultural evolution. They teach us to step back and consider how we view warfare, environmental destruction, the use of ideology, social aspects of language and texts, exploitation of labor, dominance and submission, the political and economic roles of women, the use of art."

Wendy, conversely, encouraged us to learn from what the Maya did right. How, we should ask, were they able to inhabit one of the harshest terrains imaginable and flourish for fourteen centuries? (The United States is beginning to show wrinkles after a scant 200 years!) I believe that the Maya possessed eight insights, insights that all successful civilizations understood at some level, insights from which we would do well to learn:

**1. Art builds civilizations** — If we accept "civilization" as good, then we must accept art as good, too. The Maya painted frescoes using turquoise green, yellow, and crimson pigments; created a writing system of dizzying intricacy; and built towering monuments of symmetric perfection. (The royal courtyard at Palenque, along with Picasso's Guernica and Gaudi's Familia Sagrada, is on the list of UNESCO's ten greatest masterpieces of all time.) Art was central to Maya life. Every sculpture, ceramic vessel, musical instrument, or ordinary building represented their most sophisticated technological means of communicating with the supernatural, who might then be persuaded to bestow prosperity. Maya art was the civic cement, a source of pride that drew people to cities and compelled them to work together and defend what they created. If the Maya kings' genius lay in their ability to harness the social energy, then art was one of their most powerful tools.

**2. Recognize a higher power** — The Maya's intricate cosmology explained everything from ecological systems to celestial movements. Gods gave their lives meaning and inspired them. The Maya achieved the degree of greatness they did because people subscribed to ideals higher than themselves or earthly politics.

**3. Family is a potent source of power** — Settlement pattern studies throughout the Maya area often show several structures clustered around a central courtyard. This suggests that the Maya lived in tightly knit extended families. Fathers brought their sons into the corn fields; women taught daughters how to weave and make tamales. When a special ancestor died, he or she was often buried directly under the house and was thus an ongoing source of spiritual energy. Kings took this notion to an extreme. When a Maya king took power, he often ritually destroyed his predecessor's temple and built his own over it. This, in effect, "stacked" spiritual energy and made these temples enormously powerful places. In a different but equally powerful ritual, kings would commission artwork that depicted them with great ancestors. This practice probably had the added effect of rejuvenating the king's popularity.

133

*Wendy Ashmore.*

**4. Distribute wealth fairly** — Maya subjects believed that through their kings, they could win favor with the gods. As long as the king's intervention with the gods yielded bountiful harvests and subjects were party to festival (such as, perhaps, spectacular bloodletting ceremonies), they submitted to the king's demands of building a civilization. Things fell apart when that dynamic changed. In Copán, for example, a top-heavy elite started consuming more than their share; in places like Xunantunich, the aristocracy built hidden courtyards to exclude normal citizens from ceremonies. The Maya civilization held together only as long as the people felt they shared in both the demands and rewards. When that broke down, people voted with their feet, simply leaving the civilization to crumble.

**5. Practice sacrifice** — Sacrifice plays a role every religion. The Muslims have Ramadan; Jews, Yom Kippur; and Catholics, Lent. The Maya practiced sacrifice to an extreme. Men, especially kings, periodically pierced their penises with stingray spines; women drew barbed cords through their tongues. This may strike us as bizarrely masochistic, but is it any stranger than Christ's brutal crucifixion? That single act of piety cemented a following for nearly 2,000 years. The Maya kings understood this. For them, and their subjects, sacrifice instilled discipline to endure the hard times and, during good times, a reminder that they must give back to the earth as well as receive from it.

**6. Harness spiritual energy** — Science constantly reminds us that its unique way of understanding the world is better and more true than anything else. This is not necessarily true. Maya art, religion, astrology, calendar, and medicine are all rooted in the Popol Vuh — a creation tale that involves salvation of mankind by twins, who after their immaculate conception by a skull that spits into a maiden's hand, are born and grow up to defeat evil gods of the underworld in a ball game. Bizarre as it sounds, this belief system served the Maya — and served them well — for at least 1,100 years. Some aspects of human knowledge simply can't be explained by Western science. The MayaQuest team watched as Shaman Don Pablo treated a man complaining of a piercing earache and dizziness. It involved using candles, divining crystals, nine cups of fermented "balche," and a sacrificed chicken to call upon the same nine gods mentioned in the Popol Vuh. Seven hours later, when Don Pablo packed up his charms, the man was cured.

**7. Make life hell for the ruler** — For the early Maya, combat fought largely by kings and chosen warriors kept the balance of power among rival city-states in check. Death and destruction were held at a minimum. When this changed and rules governing combat broke down, warfare began to involve peasants and farmers. Cornfields turned into battlefields and a disrupted agricultural cycle resulted in massive starvation. Life worked better when it was mainly the king's neck on the line: He thought long and hard before instigating a battle.

Our presidents and leaders engage in political battles exposing themselves to nothing more dangerous than a press conference. They send nineteen-year-olds to fight the real wars. Not only was the Maya king on the battlefield until the day he died, but he pierced his tongue and penis at every major ceremony. "Can you imagine how many Clintons we'd have," Linda Schele once said in an interview with *Omni* magazine, "If, at every important event, he had to drop his pants and push a great needle through his dick in public?" The point here is that the job of Maya king required a moral fiber and commitment level rarely seen in modern leaders.

**8. Maintain our reciprocal relationship with the Earth** — If you take a stalk of corn with all the shucks on the outside and stick it in the ground, it will not grow. It requires a human to pull off the shucks and plant the seeds. Our world view and our science says that we make that corn grow; the Maya would say that is true, but humans can't live without eating corn. This sets up a reciprocal relationship in which humans are part of the earth's system but not its owner. This attitude fosters a respect for land that perpetuates it. For generations, the Maya used ingenious but labor-intensive methods for growing their foods—including digging raised fields out of swamps and planting crops that grew within uncut forests. For some reason, the Maya abandoned these practices. At roughly that same time, there civilization collapsed.

These insights are by no means a complete summation of Maya wisdom. The Maya and their legacy offer us a palpable connection to the past and a potent vehicle to examine not only our world but our souls. Exploring the Maya world is an intensely individual experience, and everybody emerges from it with slightly different revelations and conclusions. It's like peering in a mirror—especially for the first time—everyone sees a different reflection but no one can walk away from the experience unchanged.

*The above insights were compiled from interviews and personal correspondence with dozens of Mayanists. The author would like to extend a special thanks to Wendy Ashmore, Sam Edgerton, David Freidel, Nikolai Grube, John Hoopes, Patricia McAnany, and Linda Schele.*

# ONLINE EXPERTS

**Ed Barnhardt** is a graduate student at the University of Texas at Austin. He is studying archaeology and epigraphy, specializing in Maya hieroglyphs.

**George Bey III, Ph.D.,** teaches at Millsaps College in Jackson, Mississippi. He is the head archaeologists at the Ek Balam site in Mexico.

**Christopher D. Dore, Ph.D.,** is a research associate at the University of Nebraska State Museum.

**Samuel Y. Edgerton, Ph.D.,** was a Renaissance historian until 1986, when he spent his Christmas vacation in Oaxaca, Mexico. He is currently vice president of the University of Pennsylvania Museum Precolumbian Society.

**David Freidel, Ph.D.,** is a Maya archaeologist excavating at the site of Yaxuná in Yucatan. He is a professor at Southern Methodist University in Dallas, Texas.

**John Hoopes, Ph.D.,** is an assistant professor of anthropology at the University of Kansas. He has studied the Maya with such prominent archaeologists as Michael Coe and Arthur Demarest.

**Linda Schele, Ph.D.,** is one of the world's leading Maya epigraphers, a vocation she came upon while working as an art teacher. She and David Freidel have co-authored two books on the Maya.

**Legend**

- — · — International boundary
- — · — State boundary
- • City
- ☆ State capital
- ★ National capital
- ▲ Ancient Mayan city
- ═══ MayaQuest route

DZIBILCHALTUN
Mérida ☆
START
CHICHÉN ITZÁ
Cancún •
COBA
Cozumel
UXMAL
Yucatán
LABNA
TULÚM
Campeche ☆
Quintana Roo
Bay of Campeche
Campeche
BECÁN
CHICANA
XPUJ IL
Chetumal ☆
HORMIGUERO
CALAKMUL
Hondo River
Tabasco
MEXICO
Caribbean Sea
Villahermosa ☆
EL MIRADOR
RIO AZUL
PALENQUE
END
Belize River
Belize City •
TIKAL
Belmopan ★
XUNANTUNICH
YAXCHILÁN
Usumacinta River
Lake
Petén Itza
BELIZE
Chiapas
BONAMPAK
CARACOL
Tuxtla ☆
Gutiérrez
Sarstún River
GUATEMALA
San Pedro Sula •
Lake Izabal
QUIRIGUA
Quezaltenango •
Motagua River
Copán •
HONDURAS
Guatemala •
Tegucigalpa ★
PACIFIC OCEAN
San
Salvador ★
EL
SALVADOR
NICARAGUA

N
W   E
S

0    50    100 miles
0    50    100 kilometers